AUNTIE MEDUSA
·AND·
ME

A MESSAGE FROM CHICKEN HOUSE

My favourite demigod Livi is on another madcap adventure with her Roman family, but this time it'll be hair-raising (literally). With ancient history and a whole host of gods and mythological creatures, you're in for a funny and really rather fascinating ride!

BARRY CUNNINGHAM
Publisher
Chicken House

PS: There's a super-helpful glossary on page 233 (if a word is in **bold**, the definition will be in there)!

MARIE BASTING

Chicken House

2 PALMER STREET, FROME,
SOMERSET BA11 1DS

First published in Great Britain in 2024
Chicken House
2 Palmer Street
Frome, Somerset BA11 1DS
United Kingdom
www.chickenhousebooks.com

Chicken House/Scholastic Ireland, 89E Lagan Road, Dublin Industrial Estate, Glasnevin, Dublin D11 HP5F, Republic of Ireland

Cover design by Steve Wells
Cover and interior illustrations by Flavia Sorrentino
Typeset by Dorchester Typesetting Group Ltd

ISBN 978-93-5471-848-9
This reprint edition , October 2024
Printed at Acme Print o Pac Pvt. Ltd. Noida

To Mark and Dylan,
my very own mythic heroes xx

Also by Marie Basting

Princess BMX
My Family and Other Romans

FRIENDS, ROMANS, COUNTRYMEN – HIYA!

Hi, I'm Silvia, an ordinary kid just like you. Or at least I was ordinary until my dad went missing and we both wound up back in an alternative version of Ancient Rome called Romana. Yeah, it took me by surprise too, but travelling back in time was nothing compared to what happened next. You see, it turns out I'm a demigod – daughter of the war goddess Bellona – and I have shedloads of godly brothers and sisters. Just name your favourite mythical creature and I'm probably related to them.

So, maybe I should have seen this coming. But Medusa – my Auntie Medusa? Like, what the gods!

CHAPTER 1

WEEKEND WORLD HOPPING

Tunic – check!

Palla – check!

Ten packets of Turkey Twizzlers – check!

I was all set to visit Romana.

'Livi,' called Dad from the living room, 'what on earth are you doing in there? Come on now!'

Oops. That was the third time Dad had told me

to hurry up. Extracting the remains of yesterday's packed lunch from my satchel, I crammed in the Turkey Twizzlers and slammed the freezer door shut. I raced out of the cluttered kitchen and began the usual hunt for my coat. 'Sorry, Dad.'

'OK, love,' he replied, glancing at the pendulum clock over the stone mantel. 'It's just, I was supposed to meet Chitra and the boys ten minutes ago.'

Chitra is Dad's new girlfriend. His eyes go all glossy at the mere mention of her and I've never known him to clean his teeth so much. Which can only mean one thing. KISSING. Yuck! Don't get me wrong. I'm happy for him. He deserves someone nice after my mum turned out to be a bloodthirsty war goddess, and it means I don't have to worry about him being lonely when I'm in Romana. But, really, do him and Chitra have to be quite so lovey-dovey?

'Oops,' he continued, retrieving my coat from underneath the pile of washing he was supposed to put in the machine. 'Sorry, love. Big tidy-up when I get back from town, all ready to put up the Christmas deccies.'

I wasn't holding my breath. Dad's not exactly known for his housework. Which is fine. What he lacks in furniture polish and clean socks he makes up for in being an awesome dad. Though it would be nice if he remembered to wash my underwear every now and again. I used to do more of the chores myself. But it's hard to run a house and a realm.

Outside, Mrs Burden, our next-door neighbour, was in her garden catching snowflakes on her tongue. The bubbling spring next to her giant inflatable snowman made a gurgling noise as she turned towards us and sighed.

''Asn't tasted right since the eighteenth century, this stuff,' she said, folding her arms over her flowery housecoat. 'But what can you do? Me waterworks are all over the place.'

I smiled and leant over the drystone wall to stroke Kevin, the Burdens' dog. He was wearing a pair of novelty reindeer antlers which flashed in sync with the hundreds of fairy lights dangling from the trees. I've learnt the hard way that Mrs Burden doesn't actually want an answer to her questions. It's a goddess thing. They all think they know best.

Yeah, you heard right. Mrs Burden is a goddess too. The Celtic goddess of springs and wells, to be exact – **Coventina**. She's also in charge of looking after the gateway that connects our world to Romana. Just goes to show, you can't judge a person by their foam rollers.

'Livi!' Dad was getting annoyed now. It used to be me waiting for him all the time, but since I'd discovered Romana, I was finding it hard to keep on top of everything. Legging it across the gravel drive, I climbed into the truck beside him. The engine grumbling, we pulled away from our ramshackle cottage and on to the road. The snow-peaked slopes of Whin Sill loomed above us as we passed through the tiny village of Once Brewed.

'Are you sure you'll be OK?' said Dad. The snow was really coming down now. It wouldn't be long before it stuck to the roads too.

'Of course.' I pulled my hat over my ears and turned up the heater. I wasn't about to let a bit of snow stop me visiting my brothers and sisters.

Dad wiped the condensation from the window with an old *Lord of the Rings* T-shirt and sighed. 'But the weather's really closing in up there.'

'I'll be fine.' Seriously, if I could fight off griffins and fly halfway across Romana on an overly excited metal wolf, I could make it up the hill to **Hadrian's Wall**. Turning the stereo up – Nirvana again! – I picked up the half-eaten packet of gum in the cup holder. 'Want some?'

Dad wrinkled his nose. 'No thanks. That stuff tastes like plumber's putty.'

I shrugged and put the rest of the packet in my satchel to share with my brothers and sisters. I suppose it *was* a bit stale, but they'd love it! Just like they loved the Rolos and Jammie Dodgers I took them last weekend. They couldn't get enough of the gifts I brought them from Britannia – their name for our side of the gateway.

Dad pulled up in the passing lay-by just below

Hadrian's Wall. You've heard of it, right? The super-long wall stretching across northern England that once marked the edge of the Roman Empire. The gateway was just a short walk along it, towards Housesteads Roman Fort.

'So, I'll meet you here at 3.30,' Dad said. 'Don't forget, I need you to entertain the twins for me tonight.'

As if I could forget. It was Chitra's birthday, and he'd been banging on about me looking after her sons, Ari and Avi, for weeks. 'Yes, Dad,' I said, tightening the lace on my leather **calceus.** 'You've only asked me, like, three thousand times.'

Dad laughed and leant in for a hug. 'Well, be good,' he said.

'And if you can't be good, be careful.' Squeezing each other tight, we repeated the punchline together. Proper cringey, right? But it's one of our things. Like hot chocolate in our PJs on rainy winter mornings, or crisp sandwiches for tea on long Friday-night drives to our favourite Live-Action Role-Play – ***LARP*** – events. It's what we do.

*

The carpet of snow cloaking Whin Sill was proper thick now. Almost at the wall, I picked up pace. But then I noticed Dad was still parked up in the lay-by. I waved my arms at him like I was shooing sheep. 'I'm OK.' I mouthed. 'Go!'

Dad beeped the horn and continued down the hill. I suppose you can't blame him for worrying after everything that's happened. Especially with that **Janus-faced** Athene Noctua still on the loose. She was supposed to be my mentor, but the feathery fiend betrayed me and who knows where she is now. That's why Uncle Vulcan fitted the keystone. A kind of lock that only opens for the people it recognizes. Wherever the owl lady was hiding, she wasn't getting back into Romana from Britannia.

But that didn't stop her haunting my nightmares. That's how she used to visit me, you see – in my dreams. She could read my thoughts, too, and not just when I was asleep. Yeah, I was no stranger to Athene Noctua and her big beaky gob turning up uninvited, but these latest nightmares where she lurked silently in the shadows, watching my every move, were particularly disturbing.

Reaching the stile that marked the location of the keystone, I pushed Athene Noctua from my mind and whispered the password that would awaken the magic.

Nothing.

'*Come on, come on*,' I said into the icy wind that tugged at my hair. I was totally freezanche and I could do without the stone having one of its blips. I repeated the password.

Yes, finally! The keystone glowed amber. I placed my hand flat against its warm surface and it began to flash. Excitement bubbling in my stomach, I waited for the familiar thunder . . .

Right on cue! The roar was loud enough to wake up **Somnus.**

The thunder was followed by lightning – a blinding turquoise light that split the sky in two. I gripped my satchel as the world turned black.

And then there it was, shrouded in mist and

flanked by a pair of giant blazing cauldrons, the towering triumphal arch that formed the gateway between the realms.

It was time to return to Romana.

CHAPTER 2

THE NEW ROMANA

The gateway spat me out at the edge of the city, near the familiar row of open-fronted taverns where purple-caped Praetorian Guards – the elite soldiers of the Roman army – ate lazy breakfasts of pancakes and porridge. I pulled the palla out of my bag and wrapped it around me. Covering my head, I made my way down the long straight road that led to the **forum**. The city was getting ready for the **Saturnalia** festival and the cries of hawkers selling decorative garlands, candles and **sigillaria** rose above the usual street noise.

Bad move not taking my coat off before I put the cape on. It was winter in Romana too, but it felt more like spring, and I was hotter than one of those poor horses that had to pull Sol the sun god's chariot. But I was just going to have to deal with it. I couldn't be doing with the locals throwing themselves at my feet again – which they absolutely would do if they saw my *other world* clothes.

I'm not being big-headed, but I'm a bit of a celebrity in Romana. What with the whole prophecy thing and me shooting my war-goddess mother with a sacred arrow and turning her into a baby. Which I know sounds extreme, but honestly it was the only way to stop her killing Dad and taking over the world. You're judging me, aren't you? Fair enough, I suppose, but you try stumbling across an alternative world and being told you're the chosen one. The Undecided, they call me here

– the one who would determine the fate of Romana . . . if I could just make my mind up about who to trust. Anyway, that's a different story. We best get back to this one.

The streets were heaving. Men in woollen winter capes queued at stone-countered thermopolia – the Roman equivalent to Greggs – while children played marbles with walnuts and polished pebbles outside brown-brick apartment blocks, totally oblivious to the stench of the open drains. That's something else you should know about Romana. It stinks. My twin brothers Romulus and Remus were on it, though. That's why I'm here today. The **senate** is passing their new sanitation bill. It's all been agreed, but the senators still have to vote it through officially. No tyrannical emperors here – finally, Romana is a proper democracy.

And, yeah, I know, working on a Sunday – rubbish, hey! But the Romans didn't do weekends. Still, what they lack here in lazy Sunday mornings they make up for in festivals, and Saturnalia is the biggest festival of them all.

Approaching the forum, I soon forgot about the smell. It didn't matter how many times I'd visited Romana, the mahoosive piazza with its arched **basilica**, looming marble temple and columned senate house always took my breath away. But what I loved most about it was the *Uncle Vulcanisms* – the quirky details my uncle created, like the carved bronze shop shutters, whirring dragon weather-vane and mechanical water features. I paused to take it all in . . .

'Silvia!'

Romulus. He was standing under the red-roofed **portico** of the senate house, his snake hair swaying excitedly. Oh yeah, I forgot to tell you he was a gorgon. As well as having a scalp full of serpents, him and Remus are the same colour as a duck egg and have to wear goggles so they don't turn everyone to stone!

'Come, sister,' he continued. 'The senate are waiting!'

What? The senate never ran on time. Using a

sundial or water timer made punctuality a tad difficult. As did the fact the Romanans couldn't seem to decide on how long an hour was.

Quickening my pace, I fought my way around the group of freshly bathed and oiled men gossiping on the steps to where Romulus was waiting under the legendary shield of **Minerva.** The shield had been embedded into the marble facade, where its infamous Medusa amulet guarded the city against evil. It made, like, zero sense. But that's the ancient world for you. In life, Medusa had been labelled a monster, but in death she was a protector.

'Make haste, sister,' repeated Romulus. 'The senate awaits.'

'Nice to see you too!' I said, bowing at the Medusa amulet before giving my brother a hug. Linking arms, we made our way into the lofty extension at the side of the senate chambers. 'But I thought we were going to have brunch before the meeting?'

Romulus's snake hair drooped. 'Sorry, sister.

Did you not receive my message? The senate have requested we bring the meeting forward. They are keen to break for Saturnalia. I am so excited to be seeing these changes through. It really is a historic moment for Romana.'

'OK,' I said, rummaging in my bag. 'Just let me get rid of Uncle's Twizzlers and we'll head in.'

'Thank you, sister.' Romulus signalled to one of the purple-caped guards, who scurried across the mosaic floor towards us. 'Please have someone transport these to the temple **domus**,' he said. He threaded his arm through mine again and guided me past the ten-foot statue of Bellona towards the chambers. 'I am afraid Uncle won't be joining us in the senate today. He's had to take Scylla to the dentist before everything closes down for the festival. He's taken Felix and Poly with him to distract her. She was in a terrible temper this morning.'

Wow! Brave dentist. My sister Scylla was a sea monster with six heads. And if you think that's odd, my other sister Poly is a toddler cyclops and my brother Felix can shapeshift into a **harpy**.

'Well, I don't suppose it matters,' I said, squeezing Romulus's arm. 'The senators were really behind this. And if anyone votes against it, you can always turn them to stone.'

Romulus's snake hair sniggered. The twins would never use their powers for their own ends.

'I'm so glad you are here, sister. We should get cook to whizz us up some honey cake and start the Saturnalia celebrations early. We can stay up all night and see the first hours of the festival in together.'

'I told you, Romulus. I can't stay. I have school tomorrow.'

'But you'll miss the pig sacrifice.'

Erg, I think I can live with that.

'And the games!' Romulus's snakes stood up in alarm. 'There's to be a special archery tournament in your honour before the public banquet.'

'Seriously, I'd love to stay but Dad will go ballistic if I miss any more school. I'm already on a written warning.'

Which seemed unfair. How was my attendance

record more important than running a realm? And I really was worried I might have caught smallpox the last time I called in sick.

'Forget your plebeian school,' said Romulus. 'You can learn here in Romana with me, under one of our great masters. And nobody will care if we play hooky from time to time.'

Play hooky? My brother really was the cutest. We were right at the mouth of the chambers now. Hundreds of senators in purple-trimmed togas crammed together on the tiered stone benches. At the far end of the lofty room stood the Altar of Victory and its statue of Bellona. It was a total rip-off of the Roman Altar of Victory, in the original Ancient Roman senate house, only Bellona had had the sculptor replace **Victoria** with herself.

'And what about Dad?' I whispered.

'He can move to Romana too.'

Nice idea, but I could never ask him to do that. Especially now he was dating Chitra. 'Dad loves you all, but he has his own life,' I said. 'Our home is in Britannia.'

'Poppycock, sister.' Romulus's snake hair stared at me with black beady eyes. 'The new Romana welcomes all! You made the slogan up yourself. Please stay for the festival. It will be rubbish without you.'

CHAPTER 3

NAPPY BOMB

I try not to be paranoid, but the hush passing through the senate chambers as I walked in with Romulus was enough to make Narcissus doubt himself. I was never going to get used to the way people stared at me here. No wonder Prince Harry moved to America. Thankfully, my brother Tiber broke the silence.

'Silvia, dude!' he called, waving excitedly. I waved back and he did his happy trot, his hooves clattering on the marble floor. And, yes, I did say hooves. Didn't I tell you Tiber was a centaur? Next to him, sitting on a jewelled bronze throne, was Remus, his snake hair hissing a welcome. He had one hand on the special golden crib Uncle Vulcan had made for baby Bellona. I picked up pace, hugging my brothers before leaning over the crib. 'Hello, Mum,' I said.

Bellona answered by burping in my face. A really stinky burp that could have taken a cyclops out. Still, at least she wasn't crying for once. I'd even go so far as to say she looked adorable with her chubby cheeks and yellow babygrow.

'Silvia,' smiled Remus, nodding towards the senators. 'Maybe we should make a start?'

Like, what? Can't a girl say hello to her family without everyone staring at her? I nodded back, locking eyes with **Crassus** – Bellona's former **consul** – as I scanned the benches. He smiled and bowed his bald head.

Romulus stood up. 'Friends, Romanans, country-men, lend me your ears.'

Cringetastic or what! I knew I shouldn't have lent him Dad's copy of *Julius Caesar*.

'As you know,' he continued. 'This is a historic day for Romana as we gather here to pass our groundbreaking sanitation reforms—'

Crassus raised his hand. His fingers were loaded with super-blingy rings, and he wore a heavy gold necklace that must have weighed as much as he did. He was said to be the richest man in Romana and was known for living it large. 'If I may be so bold as to interrupt,' he said, 'but before we proceed, I feel it is my duty to advise you of some concerns that have recently emerged about the bill.'

And, yep, he was also known as a troublemaker. Especially since he'd been demoted to the benches. You know the sort, right? You might even have one at your school – that Janus-faced meanie who talks about you behind your back and then pretends to be your best friend. Well, that's Crassus. He gets away with it because he throws good parties and is generous with his flamingo tongues. And because as much as we all wanted things to be different in the new Romana, thousands of years of corruption and treachery were pretty hard to stamp out.

'Of course,' said Romulus. 'Please speak.'

'I'm afraid there are rather a lot of comments,' Crassus continued. 'I have had them logged so you might peruse them at your leisure.' He nodded at one of the clerks, who stepped outside the room before returning with a creaking wheelbarrow full of scrolls.

'But I don't understand,' said Romulus, his snake hair drooping. 'We developed these changes in full consultation with the house. All that was left was to vote through the bill.'

'It is, I agree, most unfortunate that these concerns should have come to light at such a late stage, but I would hate for implementation to fail because of a lack of consultation.'

Sure he would. He was playing games again.

'A lack of consultation?' said Remus. 'As my brother outlined, there has been full opportunity for anyone who so wished to contribute.'

'Indeed,' said Crassus, scanning the benches. 'But I am sure you are aware that your divinity can make it slightly difficult for us mere mortals to speak up.'

'Dude,' said Tiber. 'These guys put the d in democracy.'

'Of course,' said Crassus. 'Which is why it is my duty, as their loyal servant, to assist the democratic process.'

Romulus's snakes were now as limp as a breadstick that had been soaked in water. Sensing his mood as only a baby goddess can, Bellona began to do that high-pitched cry of hers that makes cats try to chew their own ears off. I picked her up and her face turned tomato red. Perfect timing – another nappy bomb.

Romulus sighed. A deep sigh that made his snakes poof out. 'It's OK,' I said, rocking Bellona, 'we just need to regroup. We'll work it out together.' It wasn't the first time Crassus had tried to stall things. He got a kick out of making things difficult.

Remus nodded. 'It is nothing that can't be overcome. This is what we signed up for, brother. A true democracy.'

Romulus forced a smile, his snake hair nodding. 'Thank you, Crassus,' he said. 'You are indeed right to raise this. We must take time to consider the views of the people. As such, the senate is now adjourned for Saturnalia.'

CHAPTER 4

THE RING

Oh my gods, maybe I should move to Romana because, right now, Once Brewed was the last place I wanted to be. I knew I shouldn't have let Ari and Avi have all those Skittles. They were so full of sugar they were practically sweating syrup!

'Never mind, Ari,' I said, using a tea towel to mop up the milkshake he'd spilt. 'No harm done.'

Ari continued to stare at the telly. Chitra had said no more screens after 6 p.m. but *Arthur Christmas* had been the only way to get the twins to stop badgering me to get down on my hands and knees and pretend to be Little Donkey. It had been funny at first, especially the way they insisted on wearing tea towels on their heads to make them look like Mary, but after the zillionth time circling the room while they took it in turns to sit on my back singing about Bethlehem and the dusty road, not so much. Seriously, I was so tired I couldn't even eat the takeaway pizza Dad had ordered us. And it had extra pepperoni on it too!

I looked at the clock and groaned. How could it only be half an hour since Dad and Chitra went into the garden for their date? Dad had pitched a bell tent out there. He'd made it all romantic with fairy lights and set up the barbecue in the doorway. When Uncle Vulcan said love did strange things to people, he was not wrong. Standing around in the winter drizzle, grilling sausages over a converted oil barrel, was just ridiculous behaviour.

'I'm bored,' said Ari.

Not as bored as I was.

'Let's play Little Donkey again,' agreed Avi.

'Why don't we play a board game instead?' I forced a smile. It wasn't their fault the senate meeting had left me feeling so blah. I just hoped Romulus was OK. He'd been so upset about the sanitation bill not going through, but we'd all agreed there was nothing we could do until after Saturnalia.

'Board games are rubbish,' said Ari.

'Well, how about we play *Mario Kart*? Where's your Switch—'

'Pretend games are better!' Avi climbed down from the dining chair. He picked up his foam sword and leapt on to the battered sofa. Ari laughed and jumped on to the coffee table, waving his arms to steady himself on the slippery surface.

'Careful, Ari!' I said.

Avi jumped down from the sofa and charged towards me, whacking me with his sword. 'Naughty donkey!' he yelled.

Seriously, it was going to be a long evening.

*

'Ari! Avi! What are you doing up there?' Mmm, maybe suggesting the twins go and play upstairs while I cleared up was a bad idea. I had no clue what that bang was, but it didn't sound good.

Legging it up the stairs, I found Ari bouncing on Dad's bed with a tea cosy on his head. Like, what? I didn't even know we had a tea cosy. But, anyway, the tea cosy wasn't the issue . . . the wardrobe was. It had tipped over somehow and was resting precariously against the bed frame.

'Off the bed, Ari! Now!' He must have sensed the urgency in my voice because for once he did as he was told. 'Where's Avi?'

'In there.' Ari whacked the wardrobe with his sword. In his other hand he held a small leather box. 'Lightning bolt,' he called, chucking it at me then quickly picking it up again.

'Avi! Avi, are you OK?'

'That was brilliant,' said a muffled voice from inside the wardrobe.

Well at least he didn't seem to be hurt. 'Brilliant?!

What were you thinking? One of you could have been killed.' I climbed on to the bed and, hands flat against the smooth dark oak, pushed against the wardrobe. But the wardrobe was almost as stubborn as the twins.

'Brilliant!' repeated Avi. 'I moved the wardrobe with my mind. Like Baby Yoda!'

Yeah, right! I had half a mind to leave him in there so he couldn't cause any more trouble, but the groan from the bed-frame was not good. Using my shoulder like a bulldozer, I pushed again, harder.

The bed groaned again, this time with relief as I eased the wardrobe upwards off the footboard.

'I need a poo,' said Avi.

I continued to push. But I wasn't strong enough. I just couldn't tilt the chock-a-block wardrobe all the way back.

'Let me out!' cried Avi.

'Ari, quick, go and get my dad!' Ari picked up the leather box again. He flicked the lid open. 'Ari, run!' My arms were burning, but I was too scared to lower the wardrobe all the way down in case the footboard gave way and it fell on top of me.

'I need a poo now!' Judging by the smell drifting from the wardrobe, Avi was not lying!

'Hang in there, Avi,' I said. 'Ari, go on! Run!'

Ari put the box down on the dresser. The lid was open and inside I could see a ring . . .

. . . an engagement ring?

'Now!' cried Avi.

Yep, it was definitely an engagement ring – a mahoosive emerald engagement ring with diamonds set around the huge square-cut stone. My insides felt as dead as my arms. Where had the ring come from? Surely it wasn't for Chitra? Her and Dad had only been seeing each other for a few months. An image of my new life, constantly being forced to pretend I was a donkey, spun around my head.

Please.

No.

Don't.

Let.

It.

Be.

For Chitra.

What was Dad thinking? Didn't I have enough brothers and sisters already—

'Poo! Now!' screamed Avi.

'Just hang on one more minute. That's a good boy.'

My nostrils crinkled.

'Too late,' said Avi as Dad finally appeared in the doorway. 'Number two in my pants!'

CHAPTER 5

CRINGE MAJOR!

No! No! No! You had to be kidding me, right? That couldn't be Romulus at the classroom window. Except it was. All togged up in his bright-purple **synthesis**, the garment of choice for Saturnalia. What did he think he was doing?

'Livi!' Mr Boon, the world's strictest teacher, folded his arms. 'I said turn over your test paper.'

Yeah, I know. A test paper in the last few days of term – how tight! No watching *The Muppet Christmas Carol* and doing Secret Santa with Mr Boon. I nodded and turned over the sheet. Acids and alkalis, in case you're wondering. Straightforward enough – if your gorgon brother isn't watching you through the window. I glanced sideways again. Romulus's snake hair danced as he pointed towards the emergency exit. Was he for real? As if I could just get up and run off in the middle of a lesson.

I sighed and tried to turn my attention back to the paper. I really didn't need this today. I was finding it hard enough to concentrate, what with all the Dad and Chitra stuff whirling around in my head. I took another peek at the window. *Doh!* I was really hoping if I ignored him Romulus might go away. But he was still there, snake hair splayed against the glass, as he frantically mouthed something I couldn't make out.

'Hey!' said Mr Boon, scurrying across the classroom.

The low bubbling anger in my chest turned to worry. Romulus really shouldn't be here. If word got out about Romana, who knew what might happen. We'd been lucky up to now – thankfully people don't want to believe in magic or myth. They prefer science and logic and elaborate excuses about taking LARP to a whole new level through groundbreaking special effects. But Dad was right about not pushing our luck after that reporter came round. My brothers and sisters were supposed to be keeping a low profile.

Thankfully, **Fortuna** was on my side today . . . because when I followed Mr Boon over to the window, Romulus was gone.

'Silvia De Luca,' said Mr Boon. 'Back to your seat, right now—'

Footsteps.

Hurried footsteps, echoing in the corridor.

'Sister!' called a flustered voice. 'Where are you?'

I covered my face with my hands as the classroom door flew open.

'Silvia! You must come at once!'

Ground. Open. Up. And. Swallow. Me. Now!

'Go away,' I mouthed. If this was about the sanitation bill, I'd twist his snakes big-style!

'Erg, excuse me young man,' said Mr Boon. 'But you can't just barge into my classroom and demand one of my pupils leave with you.' Taking a closer look at Romulus's beady-eyed snake hair, Mr Boon backed behind his desk.

'I'm terribly sorry,' said Romulus. 'I mean no disrespect, but this is a family emergency. Hurry, Silvia! You must come with me now!'

'Go away,' I mouthed. I mean, a family emergency, please! The sanitation system had been the same for over 2,000 years. Another day or two wasn't going to make any difference.

'I'm calling security,' said Mr Boon, reaching for his desk phone.

Romulus rummaged in his leather satchel and pulled out a shiny bronze orb the size of an apple. He tapped it on the table, and it made a whirring noise and began to glow, the top half of its shiny shell folding outwards like wings. Resembling a giant golden scarab beetle, it began to fly around the classroom, leaving behind a trail of canary-yellow smoke.

'I am truly sorry for the inconvenience,' said Romulus, his snakes staring apologetically at Mr Boon. 'But we'll soon be on our way.' He clicked his fingers and the orb-beetle-thingy buzzed. It circled Mr Boon's head, the smoke forming a wispy blanket around the bewildered teacher.

'Erg, sorry,' said Mr Boon into the telephone receiver. 'Everything's fine. Just a case of butter fingers.' He put the receiver down and looked at the clock. 'Come on, Year 7,' he said, 'heads down.'

'Yes, sir,' responded my classmates robotically, before turning back to their test papers.

Romulus's hair snakes did that strange hissy snigger thing they do. 'Hurry, Silvia,' he said, catching the globe and putting it back into his satchel. 'The draught won't last long, and Auntie Medusa needs your help.'

CHAPTER 6

ERG, HELLO!

Erg, hello! So, forget the sanitation bill guys, because my life had just entered a whole new level of bizarre. Just when I thought my family couldn't get any stranger, Romulus only goes and tells me we're related to Medusa! And I mean, like, *the* Medusa. You remember her, right? The famous gorgon who could turn people to stone. The very same gorgon who, after being punished by Minerva for something that was so not her fault, went to live out her days quietly in exile, so she didn't have to worry about turning people into statues.

Which she did for a while – until that so-called hero Perseus came along and chopped her noggin off! I know, right? Out of order. And like that wasn't bad enough, he then went off parading Medusa's noggin all over the shop before eventually giving it to Minerva for her shield. The very same shield that now sits above the doors to the senate house in Romana.

End of story, right?

Except it wasn't.

Because Medusa's ghost was now sitting on a garden bench in front of me, knitting. Yes, knitting, her elbows going like the clappers as she knit-one-pearled-one for Gorgonia! Which was pretty impressive, given she was little more than a ghostly shadow with no head. Honestly, I thought I'd seen it all in Romana, but this was enough to make me lose my own noggin!

I wish you could have seen her. She was your classic spooky spectre, all ethereal and transparent, the same grey monochrome as those photo filters you get on Snapchat. Only instead of the standard groaning chains, Medusa came with the clack of knitting needles, and minus a noggin. Her long, elegant body was wrapped in a super-fancy cape which fell in soft folds over her shimmering stola, just below the stump where her head should have been.

We were gathered in the garden behind Bellona's temple. That's where I live when I'm in Romana – in the temple domus along with Uncle Vulcan and my brothers and sisters. Uncle moved in after Bellona turned into a baby, to help look after her. Though it often feels like we're looking after him.

Anyway, back to the garden. There I was, squeezed into the gap on the bench between Romulus and Remus, Medusa sitting opposite me with her sisters, the Prima Gorgons. I knew

Romulus and Remus had aunties in high places but I hadn't realized they were related to Stheno and Euryale, the mythical sisters I'd read about in Dad's books. Unreal or what!

The roaring charcoal braziers threw up a thin veil of smoke between us, the flames casting a golden glow over the Prima Gorgons' youthful faces. And I mean youthful. Seriously, someone needed to bottle their face cream, because Euryale and Stheno didn't look a day over twenty-five, the thumb-sized tusks jutting out from under their upper lips just accentuating their beauty.

Yes, tusks. They're a gorgon thing. Wings, too, if they're lucky. Which is probably why poor old Medusa didn't have them . . . or at least her ghost didn't. I tried to imagine what she must have looked like in life. Judging by her sisters and her shadow, I'm going with beautiful rather than monstrous. It was those around her that turned out to be the monsters.

Which is why it was such a huge thing for the gorgons to be here. I mean, you could hardly blame them for not wanting to leave the safety of the outer provinces and their homeland, Gorgonia. They'd been treated shockingly bad by both humans and their gods. But nobody seemed to be holding any grudges. After all, like Euryale said, '*All that's history, Romulus and Remus the glue that would now bind us together.*'

Well, them and the jelly baby and Turkey Twizzler sandwiches Uncle Vulcan had been cooking up on the braziers. Stheno was throwing them down her neck like there was no tomorrow. At this rate there'd be none left for Tiber, and he loved a Turkey Twizzler. He'd taken the little ones to the public feast that was tradition on the first day of Saturnalia. It seemed a shame for them to miss out on the celebrations, plus we couldn't hear ourselves think with the bawling baby Bellona around. She'd been in a particularly bad grump today. Maybe it was the constant clacking of Medusa's knitting needles, which I have to admit was a bit unsettling.

'It's the only thing that keeps her from roaming,' explained Euryale later, when we'd done with all the **hospitium** rubbish and were ready to talk business. 'She's so agitated she won't sit still. I believe she returned to Gorgonia from the Underworld because she wants to tell us something.'

'But she can't because she's got no head,' said Stheno, her delicate wings unfolding. 'That scoundrel Perseus took it. One of your lot, he was!'

'Please forgive my aunt,' said Remus in a hushed whisper. 'I am afraid her ancient brain does not wear as well as her body.'

'Cheeky beggar,' said Stheno. 'You're not too old for the naughty step.' She turned towards Uncle Vulcan. 'As for you, Curly, hurry up with those Twizzlers.'

'Enough, sister,' said Euryale. 'That is no way to address our hosts.'

Uncle Vulcan smiled, his hair and beard one massive nest of amber curls as he opened another box of Turkey Twizzlers. He was dressed in holiday clothes too, his usual pristine tunic replaced by a bright-yellow synthesis. 'It's all groovy,' he asserted.

'As you said, we're family now.'

'Indeed, auntie,' said Romulus. 'And as family we will do all in our power to assist you. Do you have any idea why Auntie Medusa's ghost might have chosen to return to Gorgonia from the Underworld?'

'I'm afraid not. But such a ghost does not return to haunt, but rather because they are haunted.'

'It is indeed curious,' agreed Romulus. 'Auntie Medusa has long been at peace. Why return after all this time?'

'That, buttercup,' said Uncle Vulcan, wiping his spade-like hands on his pristine yellow robe, 'is the million-**aureus** question.'

'We thought there might be something in the books,' said Euryale. 'Some clue as to how these strange events might unfold.'

Romulus's snake hair chattered excitedly. 'Yes, the books,' he said, jumping up from his seat. 'The **Sibylline Books** shall guide us.'

'Absolutely,' Uncle Vulcan said, pointing his finger at Romulus and clicking his tongue.

'Which is why I've taken the liberty of inviting an old friend of mine to help us interpret them. Groovy people, please welcome Albunea, the **Sibyl of Tiburtine.**'

CHAPTER 7

DIVINE INSPIRATION

A sibyl? You had to be kidding me, right? How was consulting some ancient books going to help? Everyone knows the thing to do in a crisis is have a cup of tea. But this lot were welcoming Albunea into the courtyard like she was some sort of Hollywood A-lister.

She was dressed like an A-lister too. No holiday

clothes for Albunea! Her green palla was made of the finest wool, hair piled high in dozens of elaborate braids. On her shoulder sat a cooing wood pigeon wearing gold ankle cuffs and beak guard. But the blingy pigeon was nothing compared to the rest of her entourage.

Two waif-thin boys, dressed like forest sprites, complete with gold masks and ivy crowns, spiralled and swirled as they laid a carpet of oak leaves on the floor in front of her. A third tagged along behind, struggling to carry an elaborately carved bird cage containing a pair of clucking chickens. At the back of the procession, behind a teenage girl lugging a wicker basket, was a huge bulk of a man, dressed in a leather loincloth and **manica**. And like being kippered up like a gladiator wasn't enough of a statement, the dude was walking a tiger. A humongous tiger on a very loose lead!

'This is ridiculous,' I mumbled to myself, forgetting Uncle Vulcan had hearing like a bat.

'Come on now, cupcake,' he said. 'All that negativity is bad for the cosmos. You're going to love Albunea. As well as the trancing, she practises **augury** too. It's the birds that make her the most famous prophetess in Romana.'

Two divine interventions for the price of one – whoopy! Drifting towards us like a spectre, Albunea nodded at the servant with the bird cage, who set it down and scurried out of the way.

'Welcome, old friend,' said Uncle Vulcan, kissing the sibyl's hand. 'Cosmic to see you again. Though I'm afraid we need to get straight down to business. Have you had time to consult the books?'

'Of course, oh divine one. I came straight from Capitoline Hill.'

That's where the books are kept. In a special temple guarded by Vulcan's metal dragons.

'And the answer?'

The wood pigeon on Albunea's shoulder cooed – a gentle coo that felt like a lullaby. 'The answer to what, your greatness?'

'The answer to our dilemma. Have the books given you any clues as to why Medusa might have returned?'

Still knitting, Medusa's ghost began to pace.

'Get on with it,' shouted Stheno.

Albunea sighed. She touched the oversized emerald ring on her middle finger and my stomach flipped. It was just like the ring Dad had bought Chitra. I pushed all thought of home away. I couldn't think about that right now. I had to concentrate on what was going on in Romana.

'I'm afraid,' said Albunea, 'the answer is not straightforward. The prophecy has a few gaps.'

You don't say. The Sibylline Books had more gaps than the London Underground. That's why Vulcan had brought her here.

'But do not fear,' continued Albunea, 'the answers will come once the birds and I have sampled the ghost's aura.'

Talk about stalling!

Stheno clearly felt things needed moving along too. 'Is she going to sacrifice the chickens now or what?' she said. 'I'm starving! I can't believe nobody has offered us anything to eat.'

'Sister,' said Euryale. 'You've just eaten half a

turkey. Now shush! The sibyl needs to concentrate.'

'Bagsy a leg,' said Stheno.

Albunea pulled a face like she'd been forced to sit next to a plebeian in the bath house. 'There will be no killing of the sacred birds. Mine is a humane practice.' She turned towards Vulcan. 'Shall I continue?'

'That would be groovy.'

Albunea nodded to the girl with the wicker basket, who placed a thin gold veil over the sibyl's head and handed her a roll of papyrus. Looking up at the sky, Albunea began to cluck. Yes, I know, even the chickens were rolling their eyes . . . although they seemed a bit happier about things when she released them from their cage. Returning her clucks, they marched over to the raised border behind where Medusa was pacing, and started to munch on the roses.

Albunea seemed pleased about this. She waved the scroll above her head. Clucks transitioning to a mutter, she fell on to her knees and unrolled the papyrus. Clicking her tongue repeatedly, she placed the rough paper on the bottom of the cage and smoothed it with her hand.

'Behold!' she said, lifting the papyrus so we could see the pattern of the squashed poo and bird seed.

'What is it, Albunea?' said Vulcan. 'What have you learnt?'

Albunea's eyes shone with tears. 'Poor Medusa. Her soul is an unhappy one.'

'You don't say.' I folded my arms and glanced over at Medusa, who had dropped her knitting and transformed into a pulsating ball of angry black energy. The tiger roared, its breath rising upwards like a will-o'-the-wisp, as the flames in the cauldrons died and the garden was covered in a thin veil of frost.

'Please, Albunea,' said Euryale. 'Please help us. My sister is trying to communicate, I know she is.'

Albunea nodded. She flicked the wood pigeon, which was somehow still clinging to her shoulder, and it flew towards Medusa. They became one for a moment, the bird absorbed by the ghostly gorgon's aura before flying back towards us and doing a massive poo in the centre of the mosaic.

Albunea rushed over to the poo. Medusa's ghost kneeling beside her, she began to cluck again before pressing the papyrus over the fresh green dollop. She peeled back the papyrus and studied the latest smear, her nose so close to the pigeon poo I thought she might lick it.

'She wants her head back,' she pronounced at last. She turned and pointed her manicured finger at me. 'And she has chosen the Undecided to retrieve it.'

CHAPTER 8

WHAT THE GODS?

'Wants her head back?' I stared at Albunea in disbelief. 'Medusa's head has been sitting happily in Minerva's shield for millennia. Why would she suddenly want it back now?'

'Shoot not the messenger,' said Albunea, holding up the poopy papyrus. 'The birds do not lie.'

'That's because they can't speak,' I said. 'Being

chickens and all!'

'Your mouth falls open too easily,' said Albunea. 'But your mind is closed. Dig deep and search from within. Like it or not, you are the one she has chosen.'

Why me again? I was tired of being the chosen one. And the Undecided prophecy had said nothing about hunting for heads.

Albunea tutted. She pointed at the papyrus again. 'What do you see?'

'Pumpkin,' shouted Stheno enthusiastically. 'No, pancake! It's definitely a pancake.'

I folded my arms. 'This is ridiculous.'

Medusa's ghost began to pace, causing everyone in the garden to stare at me like it was my fault she was upset.

'Come on now, cupcake,' said Vulcan. 'Give it a shot. Auntie Medusa chose you for a reason.'

'Wheel!' blurted Stheno, clapping her hands together. 'It's a cartwheel.'

'I repeat, ridiculous.' They were acting like it was a game of Pictionary.

Medusa wrung her hands together, the tiger pacing up and down on its long chain beside her.

'No,' said Stheno. 'No. I've got it. It's a shield.'

Finally, Medusa was still.

'Minerva's shield,' said Euryale, slapping Stheno on the back. 'Good job, sister. You were always the best at party games.'

What the gods? Stheno was right – the blob of poo and bird seed looked just like the shield that hung over the bronze doors of the senate house . . . except slap bang in the middle, where Medusa's head should have been, there was an empty space.

I nodded at Medusa, which was probably a bit insensitive given her situation, but she didn't seem to mind. She was already leading me towards the back door of the temple.

'Where are you going, Silvia?' said Uncle Vulcan.

'The senate house. Come on!'

'Of course,' said Remus. 'Hurry, aunties. The ghost of Medusa has spoken.'

We must have looked like a right motley crew,

pouring down the temple steps, Medusa's billowing ghost leading the way, the roaring tiger pulling on its lead just behind her. Not that the festival-goers in their brightly coloured clothes and **pilei** paid us much attention. They were all under the spell of Saturnalia, too busy feasting and dancing to care what we were up to.

Maybe that's why nobody had noticed the shield.

Even from a distance, I could tell something wasn't right. Following the tiger, I forced my way through the crowd and up the steps of the senate house to get a closer look.

'Sister?' said Romulus, hurrying up the steps behind me with Remus. He huddled in close, his shoulder melting into Medusa's ghost. 'Is it really so?'

'Yes,' I said, trying my best to disguise the panic in my voice. 'The Medusa amulet is gone.'

CHAPTER 9

CHANNELLING CHICKENS

We were back at the temple domus. The sun was beginning to set, and Uncle Vulcan had lit a fire, but I still felt cold. Cold. Frustrated. And totally useless. I paced the mosaic floor, the mouldings of Roman gods – *my family!* – staring down at me from the panelled ceiling as Lupa nipped at my heels, wanting to play.

Lupa is one of Uncle Vulcan's inventions – a giant metal wolf who can fly. And, yes, she's every bit as awesome as she sounds. Normally I loved to play with her, but right now we had a noggin to find. 'Stop it, Lupa,' I said, reaching up and stroking her copper-wire scruff. 'Go and lie down now, there's a good girl.' The wolf's fiery amber eyes glowed as she licked my hand before settling next to Uncle Vulcan, where she began to chew the leg of the **lectus**. So much for Felix's new wolf-training routine.

'Seriously, guys,' I said, throwing my arms up in frustration. 'We can't just sit around doing nothing.'

I'd promised Stheno and Euryale that we'd look after things, find Medusa's head while they returned to Gorgonia to calm their people. Word had already spread about the missing amulet and the gorgons were not happy.

Nor was Medusa. She'd become even more distressed when we'd discovered the amulet was missing. After all, she knew better than anyone just how dangerous it was in the wrong hands.

Released from the magic of the shield, it would have turned back into a noggin again – a noggin of mass destruction.

Yet there we were, sitting around waiting for Albunea to have another revelation. I couldn't bear it.

'I've told you, Silvia,' said Uncle Vulcan, knitting his fingers together behind his head and leaning back on the turquoise couch. '**Festina lente**. There's nothing to be done right now. We must wait until Albunea is able to channel her chickens again.'

Yeah, you heard him right, 'channel her chickens'. It was ludicrous, but Uncle Vulcan had insisted I wasn't going anywhere until the sibyl had further interrogated the prophecy. He'd even put extra guards on duty around the domus. He said they were to keep any uninvited visitors out, but I was one hundred per cent certain they were there to keep me in.

'Somebody must have seen something,' I persisted. 'Surely, we'd be better off asking around in the forum.'

'The Sibylline Books are the key,' said Remus, finally turning away from the wheelbarrow of scrolls from the senate house that he and Romulus had been poring over. 'The books were right about you bringing peace to Romana, and they will serve you well now.'

'Yes, chill your beans, cupcake,' said Uncle Vulcan. 'I'm sure Albunea will be back any minute. Meanwhile, why don't we put up the Saturnalia decorations?'

'*Chill my beans?* Maybe you should heat yours up. Seriously, Saturnalia decorations!'

'Well, it seems a shame to waste those wonderful garlands **Terra** gave us. And we still need to throw a die to see who gets to be king. The servants will be wondering what's going on.'

'Seriously?!' How could he even think about Saturnalia? And I'm sure the servants had enough to wonder about after a pair of gorgons flew into the garden first thing this morning.

Shaking my head, I threw myself down on the

sofa. Lupa whimpered and stood up. She put her giant metal snout on my lap and sighed.

'You sure you're OK there?' said Uncle Vulcan. 'All those negative vibes, this isn't like you.'

I shrugged. I just felt so hopeless. Hopeless and sad. And I wasn't just worried about Medusa. The truth was, the more we sat around waiting, the more I couldn't stop myself thinking about everything that was going on at home. Why hadn't Dad told me about the ring? We used to tell each other everything. The more time I spent in Romana, the more we grew apart. But I couldn't tell Uncle Vulcan about my worries. They sounded so unimportant compared to everything else that was happening. Selfish too. Dad deserved to be happy.

'Oh dear,' said Uncle Vulcan. 'The last time I saw a face that long it belonged to **Pegasus**. I think someone needs a pancake.' He smiled at the kitchen girl who was heading towards us with a bronze platter loaded with sweet treats and fruit. I breathed in the biscuity smell. Well, it wasn't going to hurt!

*

We were just finishing up the pancakes when Lupa suddenly jumped up and began to howl. The scruff on the back of her neck rigid as the bristles on a hairbrush, she rushed over to the front door, where she lowered her studded metal shoulders, ready to pounce.

'Albunea!' said Vulcan. 'Lupa can smell her tiger.'

He called Lupa to him using the new dog-training whistle he'd picked up for Felix on his last visit to Once Brewed, and stuck his giant finger up her nostril. The wolf's eyes flashed amber and she shut down.

'Better safe than sorry,' continued Uncle Vulcan. 'She's really not a fan of the feline. It's a canine thing, programmed deep into her hard drive. Not even I can interfere with the natural order of the cosmos.'

Which was weird really, given he was some sort of superdivinity. It seemed the gods all had their own strengths and talents but none of them were the complete package. It was quite disappointing, to be honest. A bit like when you really fancy fish and chips at the seaside and the chips turn out to be soggy.

I shrugged and strode over to the door, where the tiger greeted me with a roar.

The tamer tightened the chain and pulled the tiger away from the step. Poor bloke was still kippered up in his gladiator gear – he must have been freezing. He bowed and handed me a scroll. 'If I may, great Undecided, my lady sends you this.'

'What, she hasn't come with you?'

'I am afraid she is exhausted from the intervention. Everything you need is in the scroll.'

'Groovy,' said Uncle Vulcan, joining me in the doorway.

Groovy? There was a major crisis going on. The least Albunea could do was put in an appearance. 'But what if we have questions?'

'Then my mistress advises you to search harder for the answers.'

A group of rowdy men singing chants about

their favourite charioteers made their way up the narrow street towards the domus. The tiger roared and pulled on its chain.

'May I take my leave, oh divine one? I fear Cleopatra is hungry.'

'Of course,' said Vulcan, watching the tiger sniff the air. 'You can't come between a kitty and its milk.'

Tiger dude bowed his head and disappeared into the twilight. It was over to us now. I hurried back inside, Remus lighting an oil lamp as I unrolled the scroll and placed it on the writing desk.

'Like, what?! *More* bird poo?'

Fine lines had been etched into the blue-green circular poo blob, leaving an effect not unlike a rabbit warren.

'The catacombs!' said Remus. He was right – the pattern did look like the layout of Romana's underground cemetery. 'May I?' He further unwound the scroll to reveal a series of charcoal images: a goose, a spider and a strange cat-like creature with wings. Next to the cat creature there was another rabbit warren, only this one was more ordered, with the lines representing the tunnels all following a similar pattern. Right in the centre of it there was a black circle which had been marked with an X, like on a pirate's treasure map.

'Interesting,' said Uncle Vulcan, rubbing his chin. 'Very interesting.'

'But what does it mean?' I said, throwing my arms in the air in frustration. The scroll made, like, zero sense.

'It means, cupcake, it's time to bring in Coventina!'

CHAPTER 10

A RUDE AWAKENING

W*hoa! What was that?* I gasped, my eyes heavy with sleep, as I jolted upright on the bronze-framed lectus. 'It's just a dream, Livi,' I said out loud. But no matter how much I rubbed my eyes, and tried to reassure myself I was safe there in my Romanan bedroom, I couldn't chase the dream away.

It was just so real. Real and totally creepy. I was inside a giant nest. The nest was nuzzled inside a craggy hollow near the top of a snow-capped mountain but I wasn't cold. Probably because the nest was lined with soft tawny feathers and had a roaring charcoal brazier in the middle of it. A bad idea in real life, for sure, but in the dream it was awesome. Me and Dad were huddled up next to the brazier, toasting marshmallows, in our pyjamas. We were having a right laugh, talking about our plans for Saturnalia, when Dad suddenly flung me out of the nest.

But it wasn't the falling that spooked me. It was Dad's saucer-like eyes. Burning amber, they had the same unearthly wildness as an owl. A small, treacherous owl to be exact. A small treacherous owl called Athene Noctua, who may have disappeared from radar but still haunted me. Especially when I was feeling unsure about something.

Pulling the covers tight under my chin, I shut my eyes again and lay back down. I thought about cute puppies and tried to calm my breathing. It seemed just minutes since Uncle Vulcan had suggested I pop for a nap while we waited for Mrs Burden to arrive, and I wasn't ready to get out of bed just yet . . .

Double whoa! More weird dream vibes. This time it felt like there was something sitting on my chest, squeezing the breath from me. I coughed and tried to sit up. But it was no use, my shoulders were pinned to the lectus.

Gripping the sheets, I gasped as the choking sensation moved to my throat.

Something wet forced its way up my nostril!

Something wet and tickly and . . . a bit dog-breathed!

Oh my gods, Kevin! And he was smothering me with his stinky doggy kisses.

'Get off, Kev,' I said as his tongue went up my nostril again.

I loved Kevin. I really did, but there had to be a better way to let me know Mrs Burden had arrived. I just hoped she was in a better mood than when we'd called her over the brazier communicator.

Would you believe, she'd refused to come and help us until after she'd been to the bingo? Apparently, it was a big night at the Haydonian Social Club, with a weekend break in Whitley Bay to be won. Like, hello? Priorities! Still, she had at least agreed to let Dad know I was going to be stuck in Romana for a while, even if I did have to promise to clean out her chicken house as compensation for the inconvenience.

Kevin barked. He jumped down off the bed and ran to the doorway, where he turned towards me and barked again. Well, at least he had a sense of urgency.

'I'm coming, Kev,' I said, rubbing my eyes. 'Hold on.'

I followed Kevin into the atrium, where the air was thick with incense. It had been dressed for Saturnalia while I was sleeping, and looked really pretty.

And the twinkling lanterns and evergreen garlands with their bright-red berries weren't the only change. In front of the couches there was a whiteboard and a collapsible table with various random stuff on it, including a riding crop, a ruby-embossed key on a velvet cushion and a lantern which looked like it had been made out of a jam jar.

'Don't rush on my account!' Mrs Burden put the lid on her purple marker and turned away from the whiteboard, revealing Albunea's scroll with the poop blob and charcoal drawings, and the words: MISSION HEAD HEIST. She was wearing a black polo-neck jumper and ski trousers, her rigidly set hair covered by a rolled-up balaclava. Seriously, she looked like she was auditioning as an extra for *Mission: Impossible*. No wonder Uncle Vulcan was smiling. He was perched on the couch opposite her with Remus and Romulus, a jug of **nectar** and a tray of **ambrosia** cake on the low table in front of them.

'Silvia,' cried a voice from the corner of the atrium. 'I missed you!'

'Felix!' He looked extra cute today. His strawberry-blonde ringlets were pulled back in a ponytail, and he had a new gold tunic and wrist cuff. Around his neck he wore the dog whistle on a leather string. I opened my arms for a hug and, with a howling Lupa running along behind him, he flung himself at me, almost knocking me over.

'Look what Coventina gave me,' he said, showing me the ancient Walkman clipped to his belt. 'It plays music!'

'Well, nobody else wanted it,' shrugged Mrs Burden, as though she had to justify being nice. 'Now quit with the larking around and sit down, the pair of you. It's time to get down to business.'

I folded my arms. Since when was she in charge?

'And don't look at me like that, missy. Do you want my 'elp with this mission or not? Because if yer want to live past midday, you'd better listen up.'

Whatever. I squeezed into the gap between Remus and Romulus. Not because Mrs Burden told me to, mind. But because one of the servants was heading into the atrium with a jug of juice and some pastries, and they looked well nice.

'Do you like the Saturnalia decorations?' said Felix. 'Uncle let me and Poly help put them up.'

Mrs Burden glared at Felix. 'You too, turkey boy, or that might just be the last song you listen to. I shouldn't need to remind you that Medusa's 'ead has turned far bigger gods than you to stone.'

'Sorry, Coventina,' said Felix. He flopped down on the Persian rug between my feet, Lupa letting out a heavy sigh as she flopped down next to him, almost knocking the juice over with her tail.

'OK, let's go.' Mrs Burden clapped her hands together. 'So, while this one's been sleeping half her life away, me and Vulcs 'ave been working our Christmas stockings off to come up with a plan.'

For Jupiter's sake, I'd only been asleep for a couple of hours . . . hadn't I? I looked at the sand timer in the corner. The hourglass had been flipped over to mark a new day, the bottom bulb already containing a thick layer of sand. It must have been at least 4 a.m. Like, how did that happen?

'So, first off, the team,' continued Mrs Burden. 'Vulcs, now would be a good time to bring in Thelma.'

'Thelma? Who's Thelma?'

'Quiet!' With a glare that would put Medusa to shame, Mrs Burden threw her marker at my head. 'Listen up and you might just find out.'

Like, no need! Thankfully, Felix jumped up and caught the marker before it took me out. That's his talent, you see – speed. Speed and being able to transform into a harpy with laser eyes!

Uncle Vulcan clapped his hands together three times. There was a whirring noise, and something beeped behind the velvet room divider.

Remus's snake hair hissed. 'What the flamingo tongues?!'

'Meet Thelma,' said Uncle Vulcan. 'Silvia's guide.'

CHAPTER 11

TWENTY-FIRST-CENTURY GIRL!

What the flamingo tongues, indeed! Thelma was a robot. A very tall, polished bronze robot, with a physique like an Olympic weight-lifter. She was wearing a lime-green cheerleader's outfit, her neat copper-wire ponytail tied back in a bow. Eyes glowing with fire and waving a pair of purple and gold pom-poms, she whizzed towards us, Lupa knocking over the low table as she jumped up and howled her approval.

'Two! Four! Six! Eight!' Thelma jumped into the air. 'Who do we appreciate?' She paused for dramatic effect before pointing her pom-poms at me. 'Silvia!' she cried.

Smiling like he'd just been visited by **Laetitia**, Uncle Vulcan slapped his thigh. 'Groovy, hey! I was going to give her to you as a Saturnalia present – a new best friend to keep you company when you are away from your brothers and sisters – but a few upgrades and she's all ready to guide you through the catacombs.'

'Let's be friends,' said Thelma. 'Best friends for ever.'

Erg, OK.

'Say hello now, Silvia. You two are going to get along like a domus on fire. Thelma's super-groovy-intelligent, and she loves playing games.'

'Battledore,' said Thelma, holding her pom-poms above her head to stop Lupa from chewing them. 'Let's play battledore.'

'Battledore?' said Mrs Burden. 'Like this is the time for badminton. I thought you said she was mission-ready.'

'She is,' said Uncle Vulcan. 'But there's nothing wrong with a few pleasantries.'

Thelma cocked her ear. Dropping her pom-poms, she whizzed across the lofty atrium to the **impluvium**, where Kevin was trying to catch the spray from the fountain. *Like, eww.* That was our drinking water he had his mucky paws in.

Thelma wasn't impressed either. 'Danger!' she cried, dragging him out by the scruff of his neck. 'Danger!'

Lupa woofed. She ran around the impluvium in circles, howling like it was a full moon.

Felix blew the dog whistle. 'Come here, Lupa,' he called.

'In the name of Jupiter,' bellowed Mrs Burden. 'Can we just get on with the briefing?!'

Fair point. It was total bedlam. All we needed now was for my little cyclops sister Poly to wake up and start sucking everyone's kneecaps.

Uncle Vulcan grabbed hold of Lupa's collar and powered her down. 'It's OK, Thelma,' he said, continuing towards her. 'Now put the doggy down.'

Thelma was not convinced. She lifted the squirming Kevin to her mouth and started giving him the kiss of life.

Barking a warning, Kevin broke free. He legged it back towards the impluvium, where he dived into the water and lay down, only to be grabbed by Thelma again. 'Danger!'

'Oopsie!' said Uncle Vulcan. 'It would seem her drowning warning is a little oversensitive.'

You don't say!

'Thelma –' Uncle Vulcan wagged his finger at the robot – 'please put the doggy down.'

Kevin yelped in agreement, swinging like a pendulum as he fought to free himself from the robot's iron grip.

There was a super-loud crashing noise as Mrs Burden smashed the riding crop against the table. 'Enough! Thelma, move away from the dog. I repeat, move away from the dog.'

But Thelma couldn't move away from Kevin. Because her hand had seized up. 'Malfunction,' she cried. 'Malfunction.'

Vulcan scratched his head. 'Oh dear, it looks like she has a rust issue too. I knew I should have tested her more thoroughly.'

Kevin snarled angrily. He wasn't normally a snarler – he left that to Mrs Burden – but you couldn't blame him for being annoyed.

'Sorry, Kev,' said Uncle Vulcan. 'I'm on it.' He opened the storage hatch in Thelma's back and took out what looked like a cross between a fancy polished teapot and an oil can. 'Here, Silvia,' he said. 'Hold this. You may as well learn how to adjust her ichor levels.'

Ichor? The lifeblood of the gods? Taking the can from Uncle Vulcan, I stood up on my tippy-toes to get a better look as he parted Thelma's copper hair to reveal a series of flashing lights and what looked like a plastic bottle cap.

Romulus squeezed in next to me, munching on

a pastry. 'She really has ichor running through her veins?' he said.

'Well, not veins exactly,' said Uncle Vulcan, pouring the golden liquid into Thelma's neck. 'But yes, she's based on the blueprint I used for **Talos**, all those years ago. Groovy, hey?'

I suppose. Except, according to the myths, things didn't exactly end well for Talos.

'Don't worry,' said Vulcan. 'She may be retro, but she's a twenty-first-century girl through and through. She won't let you down. Not now I've balanced her ichor.'

'Let's 'ope not, Vulcs,' said Mrs Burden, staring at me like I'd just trampled mud into her new wool carpet. 'Cos this one's gonna need all the 'elp she can get. Now, can we quit messing about with robots and get back to the briefing?'

CHAPTER 12

MISSION ALMOST IMPOSSIBLE

Suited me! I'd be well happy to get back to the briefing. I'd been in the atrium for at least half an hour and the only thing I'd learnt is that Uncle Vulcan is rubbish at making robots. I reached around Felix for another pastry. May as well keep my energy up.

'When yer quite ready, I believe we were

discussing the team.' Mrs Burden flipped the whiteboard to reveal a flow chart consisting of a series of mugshots. She was right at the top of the chart, labelled HEAD-HEIST MASTERMIND. Below her, next to the label EXTRACTION TEAM there were pictures of me, Thelma and Felix. Uncle Vulcan was down for EQUIPMENT and Romulus and Remus were down as BACKUP.

'But—'

'No buts. We agreed the team when you were sleeping, so shut yer cake 'ole and listen up.'

Oh my gods! She was always bossy and obnoxious, but this was something else! Who did she think she was? Watching Secret Service and true crime documentaries hardly made her Spy Kid material, but she'd clearly convinced Uncle Vulcan she was the next best thing.

'You can't send Felix in!' I persisted. 'It's too dangerous.'

'Might I remind you, you're the one who's mortal. Felix will be 'rite.'

'Immortality didn't exactly help Atlas.' Perseus

had used Medusa's head to turn the Titan god to stone! And I was quite aware of my own mortality. I'd chosen to remain that way, after all.

'Don't worry,' said Felix. He jumped up on to the couch, his arms held out like wings. 'I'll fry anyone who tries to hurt us.'

'You listen up too, Felix – there'll be no frying anybody. Use of yer laser eyes in those tunnels is strictly prohibited. Unless yer wanting to bring the roof down on top of yer sister's 'ead!'

'Another reason why it's a bad idea for him to come.'

'I told yer, the crew's been agreed. We can't fight against the prophecy. Felix was chosen to accompany you by **the Fates**. Why else do you think Albunea drew a turkey?'

She flipped the whiteboard again, jabbing Albunea's scrawly bird drawing with her riding crop.

'That's not a turkey, it's a goose.' They didn't even *have* turkeys in Romana.

Felix folded his arms. 'And I'm not a turkey,

I'm a harpy.'

'Whatever,' said Mrs Burden. 'You'll be cold meat sandwiches if you don't stop givin' me lip.'

'Do you have to be so mean to Felix?' She was really getting on my nerves now. We were supposed to be a team. Team Help Medusa. And all this talking wasn't helping anyone.

Mrs Burden tapped her riding whip against her palm. 'It's called tough love. You both need to know what yer up against.'

'So maybe you could get on and tell me,' I said, holding her stare. 'This briefing is a joke.'

Thelma's eyes flashed amber. She waved her pom-poms in the air. 'Thelma likes jokes! Why did the robot cross the road?'

'Shush, Thelma!' The water in the impluvium began to bubble as a stormy, black cloud formed above Mrs Burden's head. Kevin whimpered and covered his eyes with his paws. 'And as for you, missy, one more comment like that and you're on yer own. Now, for the final time, everyone listen up!'

Erg, OK. No need to get all water goddess on us.

'So, while Vulcs 'as been working on equipment,' she continued, the cloud turning to mist and evaporating, 'I've been gathering intelligence.' She pointed the riding crop at the poopy blob. 'Thanks to Albunea, we know Medusa's 'ead is 'ere in the catacombs. We also know it is protected by a winged cat and a spider curse.' She jabbed Albunea's bird scrawl again. 'And that the turkey boy must be the one to 'elp Silvia.'

If you say so.

'What we don't know is who took the 'ead and why. So, Silvia, you must be prepared for the worst. There's nothing in the prophecy to suggest you will die, but it wouldn't be the first time the books 'ave been wrong.'

Well, that's reassuring. *Not.* I knew being the Undecided was not without risk, but she could have sweetened it a little.

'What of these rumours of the Collectoris?' said Remus, his snake hair staring at Mrs Burden. 'Word in the bath house is—'

'Word in the bath 'ouse! Well, word 'ere is there's no such person. If there was, I'd know about it.'

Remus's snake hair hissed. 'But they are said to have been on the lookout for new mythical memorabilia.'

'What a load of old socks. Next you'll be suggesting it was the bogeyman took the 'ead. Now, if yer don't mind, I 'ave a briefing to give.' Shaking her head at Remus, Mrs Burden pointed at the final charcoal drawing Albunea had scrawled – the one that looked like an orderly rabbit warren. 'So, yeah, we have the winged cat, spider curse and a turkey boy. What we weren't so sure about was this drawing 'ere with the X in the middle, but having run the image through Thelma's Poogle Lens, we have concluded it is a **labyrinth.** A labyrinth positioned right at the centre of the catacombs, housing an impenetrable vault.'

'And you can tell that from that scrawl?' I'd never heard anything so ridiculous in my life.

Mrs Burden's mouth was so pinched it almost disappeared. She flipped the whiteboard over for a third time. Like, what? Where did the photos go? The board was now completely blank. 'Thelma,' she continued. 'Bring up the drawing.'

Thelma beeped and a funnel of light shot from her forehead, projecting Albunea's scrawly drawing on to the whiteboard. 'Well done, lass. Now, zoom in.'

OK, fair enough, magnified that could pass for a labyrinth.

'Happy now, missy? Now, if you look closely, you'll see it's an exact replica of the legendary Labyrinth of Knossos. Well, except for the vault in the middle 'ere, where Albunea placed the X.'

'And the fact it's slap bang in the middle of the catacombs.'

'Whatever,' said Mrs Burden. 'The original labyrinth wasn't guarded by a winged cat and a spider curse either, but that's what yer up against.'

I got up from the couch and studied the charcoal drawings. Of course the labyrinth wasn't guarded by a cat or a spider, it was guarded by the minotaur . . . but I definitely recognized the winged cat creature from somewhere. Screwing my nose up in contemplation, I traced its outline with my finger. 'The Sphinx,' I said. 'It looks like the **Sphinx of Thebes**.'

'Mmm,' said Mrs Burden, studying Albunea's scribble. 'That woman really should 'ave drawing lessons.'

'So, you do think it's meant to be the Sphinx?' I hoped not. The penalty for getting her riddles wrong was death.

'I wouldn't 'ave thought so. She died millennia ago.'

'But what if she didn't? Cats have nine lives after all. And she was kind of owed one by Juno.'

Mrs Burden folded her arms. 'Well, if it is 'er, it shouldn't be a problem, should it? Not for the realm's biggest know-it-all. Now shush. I was about to tell you about the impenetrable vault.'

'Impenetrable? And how am I supposed to break into that?'

Mrs Burden picked the ruby-embossed key up off the table. 'With the **Janus** key, that's 'ow.'

I guess that could work. Janus was the Roman god of portals and doors, but Mrs Burden now guarded the gateways between the realms. Which meant she got to keep the special key that could open any doorway.

Uncle Vulcan stood up and walked towards the table. 'And as backup,' he said, 'you have my special lava breakers—'

'Not now, Vulcan! I told yer, you can cover all that later. It's boring and I need to get back for me aquafit session. My world doesn't stop for Saturnalia, like some people's.'

Vulcan sank back into the sofa. Gods forbid anyone should get in the way of Mrs Burden's hobbies.

She looked at her watch. 'So, there it is. Your route to the vault is programmed into Thelma's ichor drive. All you 'ave to do is follow the robot and not mess it up. Now, anybody got any questions before I get off?'

'Can we have some honey cake now?' said Felix. 'And maybe some of those mithai Chitra sent for us to try? It *is* Saturnalia.'

'Well, Saturn will just 'ave to wait till I'm done. Any proper questions?'

'Should we perhaps cover our role, Coventina?' said Romulus, nodding at Remus.

'What more is there to say? You and 'im are there to provide backup if *she*' – meaning me – 'messes up. We've been through this.'

'But not with Silvia. I thought she might appreciate an update on the communication lantern.'

Mrs Burden picked up her tartan handbag and looped it over her arm. 'I said yer uncle can brief the girl on kit. Now, if you don't mind, I promised Bert hot croissants and jam before I went down the leisure centre. That reminds me, Vulcs, did I give you any of that gooseberry marmalade I made?'

'No, I don't think you did, Tina.'

'I'll 'ave the girl bring some over on her next visit. If she makes it back from the catacombs, that is. Just mind there's no mould on the lid.'

I rolled my eyes. 'Seriously, is now really the right time to be talking about marmalade?'

'Anytime is the right time to talk about marmalade, lass. Now quit with the whinging. My part is done. You 'ave your plan and you 'ave your team. It's over to you lot now.'

CHAPTER 13

LET THE HEAD HEIST COMMENCE

'So, Silvia, are you sure you've got everything?' said Uncle Vulcan.

We were outside the cave-like entrance to the catacombs. Shadows danced around us in the dim light of the oil lamp and the wind whistled through the poplar trees.

'Yes, Uncle,' I said, tapping my satchel. 'I told

you, I put everything in my bag after the briefing. Though I still don't see why I need to take the socks.'

'Because it will be cold down there, cupcake. Nobody does their best work with cold feet.'

'Well, I'm not wearing the balaclava.' The thought of the catacombs was claustrophobic enough without having to cover my nose and my mouth.

'I like the hats,' said Felix, munching on a slice of honey cake. 'They make us look mysterious.'

'And Coventina was very clear. They are a key part of your kit.' Uncle Vulcan pointed towards the steep steps that led into the catacombs. 'You'd be surprised how busy it can get down there, cupcake. People like to visit their folks during the holidays.'

'Well, it was about the only thing Mrs Burden was clear about. That and the need to get home for her aquafit.'

Uncle Vulcan rubbed his beard and glanced down the deserted road. The catacombs were just outside the city walls in the absolute middle of nowhere. The only buildings nearby were the deserted shepherd's hut where Romulus and Remus had set up the brazier communicator, and a few fancy villas scattered across the distant farmland.

'Come on now, cupcake, everything is going to be fine. You're just having a little pre-match wobble. Are you doing your affirmations like I told you? Those negative thoughts won't fight themselves.'

I nodded. I sort of was. Though I'd drawn the line at doing a group meditation before we left the domus.

'OK, so let's go through the rest of the kit. First, the lava breakers . . .'

'I warm the breaker in my fingers, place it on the lock and then shut the lid on the case to detonate.'

'But only when you are clear of the vault door,' said Uncle Vulcan. 'You have fifteen seconds . . .'

'From closing the lid to detonation. I know all this. We've been through it a thousand times.'

All this fussing was doing my head in. I felt like I was perched in the open doorway of an aeroplane about to do a parachute jump. I just wanted to make the leap and get on with it. Had people forgotten this was a noggin of mass destruction we were dealing with here? Plus, I needed to get back and find out what was going on with the ring. What if Dad had already asked Chitra to marry him? The twins could be moving into my bedroom any minute.

And it wasn't just me who was growing more and more uneasy with every second we wasted – the latest word from Gorgonia was of widespread unrest. So much so, Euryale and Stheno were worried there might be a gorgon rebellion if Medusa's head wasn't found soon. The mood in Romana wasn't much better. People really believed they were in danger without the amulet to protect them, and perhaps they were – any rebellion in Gorgonia would not be contained to the outer provinces. Uncle Vulcan had instructed that the Saturnalia celebrations should continue, hoping they'd provide a distraction, but the only real way to calm people was to get the head back.

'And the goggles?' persisted Uncle Vulcan.

'Be sure to put them on before entering the vault. They'll protect us from side glare, but they won't stand a full-on stare from Medusa.'

Nothing would. Her powers were far too strong. Which was fine. I wasn't scared of the head. After all, Medusa had chosen me to help her. It was what else I might find in the catacombs that was worrying me. And the more we stood around talking, the more I had time to think about what could go wrong.

'Good girl,' said Uncle Vulcan. He handed me the communication lantern. It really did look like a jam jar – a half-empty jam jar containing bubbling apricot lava jam. 'And don't forget, you have Romulus and Remus tracking your progress,' he continued. 'The lava in the jar will send a constant signal to their brazier in the shepherd's hut. Any problems and they'll be down there faster than their snakes can hiss.'

Romulus and Remus gave me the thumbs up. But I could tell by the droop of their snakes they were worried too. After all, it was hard to put your faith in something that looked like a nursery science project – even if it had been made by a god famous for his inventions.

Lupa licked my hand. She seemed worried too, her tail hanging limply between her legs. She was wearing a barrel around her neck like a St Bernard rescue dog, Felix insisting she should wait with Romulus and Remus, as part of her training regime.

I ruffled her copper-wire scruff. 'Can we go now?'

'Yes,' said Felix. 'Let's go!' He ran to the top of the stairs and peered into the dark, narrow tunnel. 'Cockroaches,' he said. 'Cool.'

Erg!

Uncle Vulcan shrugged. 'I'm sure there won't be roaches in the tunnels. It's a bit cold for them down there.'

How reassuring! Trying not to shiver, I forced a smile and hugged the twins goodbye.

'Stay safe, sister,' said Remus, squeezing me tight.

‘I’ll be fine,’ I said. ‘Medusa chose me for a reason.’

‘Indeed, sister,’ said Romulus. ‘Your destiny is one with hers.’

CHAPTER 14

MORTAL DANGER!

So, what you need to know about the catacombs in Romana is that they were working catacombs. They weren't like the pictures you may have seen of the touristy tunnels lit up by spotlights and lined with rows of empty loculi. They were actual cemeteries. Which meant the loculi – horizontal niche-tombs cut into the volcanic rock

– contained actual dead bodies. Disintegrating dead bodies judging by the smell.

Well, some of the tombs did anyway. Others were still empty – cold narrow shelves, kind of a cross between bunkbeds and a bookcase – waiting for other family members to pop their clogs and join their loved ones. It was proper sad. Like I'd arrived in some sort of limbo.

A dark, cavernous limbo with never-ending tunnels that closed in on you like a vice. Never-ending tunnels that made strange creaking noises and were home to mysterious draughts and air pockets where the temperature would suddenly drop as though a ghost had just run its finger down your spine. And yeah, I know that sounds dramatic, but it really was proper scary. Especially for someone whose worst fear was being buried alive.

But eventually, I got used to it. Kind of. At least enough to stop feeling like there was a minotaur sitting on my chest.

'Silvia, look at this!'

My jam-jar-lantern communicator flickering, I headed towards Felix. He was slightly ahead with Thelma, the robot's built-in spotlight creating a halo effect around her body as it reflected off the domed ceiling. The rustle of her pom-poms catching against the walls set my nerves on edge. Did she really have to bring them? Vulcan said they were an important part of her identity, but still.

'Hurry up, Silvia!' said Felix. 'You have to see this.'

Oh my gods! Oh my gods! Oh my gods! A dead body. An actual dead body. It was laid out on one of the lower shelves, the red shroud it was wrapped in sprinkled with a dusting of powdered limestone. The lime was supposed to help with the smell. Which it *so* didn't. Think school dining hall on fish Fridays only a thousand times worse, and you'll kind of get the picture.

'Come away, Felix!' He was messing about with one of the clay oil lamps that had been set out on the shelf above the body, along with a bunch of narcissus and a platter of grapes. Yes, flowers and grapes – just what every dead person needed. Not.

Felix put the lamp down and crouched down next to the body, his chin practically touching the stone shelf. 'Cool!' he said. 'You can see their nose through the cloth.'

'Seriously, Felix. That's a real person. Come away.'

'Don't worry, Silvia,' he said, charging along after Thelma, who was well ahead now. 'They don't need their body any more. They've had the proper burial rites.'

Unlike poor old Medusa. Felix was right. Whoever it was wrapped in that shroud would have crossed the Styx by now. Their afterlife decided even before their tomb was sealed. We needed to help Medusa find peace too. Which was never going to happen while there was a chance of her head being used as a weapon again – the ultimate weapon, which in the wrong hands could mean doom for us all.

Picking up pace, I followed Thelma and Felix further into the tunnel, shivering as a giant spider's web tickled my head. I brushed the thick, sticky threads from my hair. There was shedloads of the stuff. And like the super-web wasn't creepy enough, there was another body up ahead. This one had clearly not been put into its tomb properly. Its foot had fallen free and was dangling over the edge of the loculus. I edged towards it, wondering if I should tuck it back in—

'Danger!' Eyes flashing amber, Thelma whizzed ahead towards a fork in the tunnel, just beyond the body. 'Unidentifiable life form detected! Switching to thermo sensor.'

Whoa!

What was that noise . . . ?

Scurrying at first.

Then squeaking.

A *cacophony* of squeaking, as an author might say, even though nobody ever uses the word cacophony in real life.

It was coming from one of the side tunnels. I reached for my sword as a shadow formed on the floor ahead.

A writhing, screaming shadow with hundreds

of glaring red eyes.

And I mean hundreds!

'Rats!' confirmed Thelma. She let out a high-pitched robotic scream – 'Arg. Arg. Arg. Arg.'

Weird, hey? A robot screaming. Though, I suppose, there were rats swarming over her feet.

A lot of rats.

Giant evil-eyed rats that tickled your ankles—

Oh my gods – there are rats tickling my ankles!

'*Arg. Arg. Arg. Arg!*' The jam jar communicator smashed against the stone shelf as I scrambled up on to the occupied loculus. It fell to the ground, the rats joining in with the screaming as they swarmed over the broken glass. Seriously, I'm all for recycling, but I knew using a jam jar for an essential piece of kit was a bad idea—

Something cold and clammy grabbed my ankle.

I jumped down from the loculus as the shrouded corpse sat up.

'Cool!' said Felix. 'Immortalis!'

The undying?! There was nothing cool about being faced with a zombie.

I gripped my sword, ready to draw. 'Show yourself!'

'Of course,' said a plummy voice. 'But would you mind awfully turning the light down first?'

Thelma adjusted her spotlight to a soft haze and a tangle of russet curls emerged from the shroud. They belonged to a short man dressed in a **toga pulla**. Smiling, he shuffled out of the loculus and removed the wax plugs from his ears.

'Rubbish,' said Felix. 'It's just a mortal.'

The man rubbed his eyes. 'By Jupiter,' he said, staring at me like I was made out of gold or something. He fell to his knees. 'All hail the Undecided!'

Uh-oh! This wasn't good. Our mission was supposed to be top secret. I figured Uncle Vulcan was being over the top when he made us pack balaclavas, but now I wished I'd worn it.

'There's no need for all that,' I said. 'Lovely to meet you, but we need to get off now.'

'Please, oh divine one, Anthony Julius Alexander at your service, merchant and loyal citizen. You must allow me to afford you some refreshment. My wife would never forgive me if I didn't provide her the opportunity to honour the Undecided. We're commemorating my deceased brother in the chamber just around the corner.'

Sandals slapped against the dusty tufa floor.

'Oh look, here's my good lady now.'

A woman with very tall poodle hair wearing a dark wool palla tottered towards us. She nodded a greeting before turning her attention back to her husband. 'Darling, everyone is waiting for you to lead the singing.'

'Let them wait a little longer,' said Anthony. 'Do you not recognize who you stand before?'

But the woman wasn't paying attention to us, her eyes were scanning the tunnel. 'Where's Flavia?' she said.

'I thought she was with you.'

Anthony's wife looked like she'd washed down a dozen doughnuts with an extra-large milkshake and then gone on a roller coaster. 'But she came to find you an hour ago!'

'I'm sure she's fine,' said Anthony, his eyes darting around the tunnel. 'She probably saw me napping and decided to rest too.'

Let's hope so. The catacombs were no place for a kid to be wandering about on their own.

'Thelma,' I said, 'scan the loculi now. You're looking for a child. A live one!'

Thelma's eyes flashed amber. 'No heat source detected.'

'Try again, Thelma. Expand your search.'

Thelma shut her eyes. When she opened them again they looked like pools of burning fire. You could feel the heat radiating from her ichor drive. 'Danger!' she said, her eyes now a whirling pool of molten red. 'Mortal danger!'

CHAPTER 15

THEM BONES, THEM BONES!

'Calm down, Thelma!' I said as I followed her down the tunnel, Anthony and his wife, Julia, scurrying behind. Seriously, why did Thelma have to be so dramatic? She was waving her pom-poms in warning and her spotlight was flashing blue like a police siren. 'Try not to worry,' I reassured Anthony and Julia. 'She can be a little OTT at times. I'm sure your daughter's fine.'

'Yes,' said Felix. 'She'll be OK. We lost our sister Scylla once and we found her in the public latrines.'

And when he says in the latrines, he means *in* the latrines. Sea monsters really are disgusting.

'Ow!' Like, thanks for the warning, Thelma. She had stopped suddenly at the entrance to one of the many side tunnels, my face slamming into her shoulder.

'Danger,' she cried, staring into the tunnel. 'Life form ahead.'

I squeezed in beside her. The tunnel was cordoned off with yellow and black police tape, the words MORTAL DANGER scrawled on the wall next to it along with a picture of someone being squashed by falling rocks. It looked like Thelma wasn't the only one being overly dramatic.

'Danger,' she said. 'Mortal danger.'

Yeah, yeah, we get the picture, Thelma.

'Heat source detected eighty-five metres ahead.'

'See,' I said, smiling reassuringly at Julia, 'your

daughter's probably just playing in the tunnel. Let me fetch her for you.' Sure, the tunnel was dangerous, but I had a reputation as a hero to live up to.

'Danger,' said Thelma, trying to block my way with her arm. 'Approach target with caution.'

'Stop being silly, Thelma. She's just a little girl.'

'Thelma first. Thelma must protect the Undecided.'

Whatever. I needed Thelma to light the tunnel anyway. 'OK, but switch to stealth mode. And be careful not to touch anything.'

This tunnel was wider than the ones we'd travelled through so far. Older too, the arched tombs – arcosolia – cut into the walls decorated with elaborate **frescoes** of animals, fruit vines and flowers. You didn't need to read the inscriptions to know this was a corridor for the rich and noble . . .

And . . .

. . .

. . . spiders!

Honestly, you should have seen the webs. They were everywhere now, the tombs smothered in a thick tapestry of silk that reminded me of the old-fashioned lace tablecloths you sometimes got in retro teashops. Sure, they were creepy, but they were beautiful too. Spidery works of art that shimmered and glistened in Thelma's spotlight. No wonder little Flavia had been curious.

'Approaching heat source,' said Thelma. 'Brace!'

Seriously, I was going to have to get Uncle Vulcan to do something about her negative and dramatic tendencies. It was like adventuring with Eeyore.

'Flavia,' I called. 'Are you there?'

A gust of wind whistled down the tunnel, the blanket of webs above me billowing like sheets on a washing line.

Thelma thew her pom-poms on the floor. 'Switching to defence mode,' she warned. 'Any attack will be reciprocated.'

'Seriously, Thelma. Cut it out, or I'll power you down.'

The robot huffed and folded her arms. It would seem she'd learnt some human characteristics more efficiently than others.

'Now, stay behind me and switch your spotlight to full beam.'

White light flooded the tunnel as Thelma traced my descent into the darkness.

'Flavia?'

The wind again. A sheet of webbing brushed my head, sending ripples of unease down my spine.

'Flavia! Don't be scared. I'm here to take you back to your parents.'

Ow! What was that? I picked up the silver sphere that had just pelted my head. It was the size of a cricket ball and just as heavy – layers and layers of super-compressed silk wound up like a ball of yarn.

Another silk ball followed. This time whacking me in the back.

'Flavia!'

A stifled giggle echoed down the tunnel.

'Come on, Thelma,' I said, following the giggle towards a doorway at the end of the corridor. *Wow! A crypt. A crypt lined with skulls!*

Yes, skulls. Human skulls!

Hundreds of them piled high on top of each other and cemented into the walls like bricks. I'd stumbled upon an **ossuary**!

In the centre of the lofty space, stretching upwards to the domed ceiling, there was a barrel-shaped sculpture made of disassembled skeletons, the bones stacked neatly on top of each other, knee and thigh joints aligned to create a nice, clean finish. It was every bit as disturbing as it sounds—

Another silk ball!

This time coming from above.

'Flavia?' I stared at the intricately weaved webs decorating the ossuary ceiling. Layer upon layer of super-strong silky curtains that glimmered, like an ice palace in the sun.

And how did I know they were strong, you ask?

Because there was a girl lying in one of them.

A girl with russet curls.

And right behind her, pedipalps twitching like Medusa's knitting needles, was a spider the size of the **Pantheon**.

CHAPTER 16

ARACHNOPHOBIA!

Well, OK, maybe not quite the size of the Pantheon, but trust me, it was a big spider. The size of a small car at least. And that was just its body. It stared down at me with mirrored eyes – all eight of them – giant fangs protruding from its drooling mouth.

'Danger,' said Thelma from the stoned archway to the ossuary. 'Unidentifiable life form.'

Unidentifiable? It was quite clearly a spider. A hairy spider with a furrowed brow that looked like it was trying to read my next move. Good luck with that, spider, because I didn't have one—

'Oh yay, how exciting!' The spider shuffled across the net of webs and pushed itself up on its fuzzy front legs. 'Two visitors in one day. This almost never happens. Not since the rumours.'

Yes, friends, a giant, hairy, talking spider. What the arachnids?

'Dangerous, they called me. A ferocious beast. Me? Ferocious? I wouldn't hurt a fly.' She pinged the giant web she was suspended in and laughed nervously. 'Well, not on purpose. Though, it can be a hazard of the job, if you know what I mean.'

'Oh,' was all I could manage before she went off on one again.

'Anyway, I'm glad the mortals stopped coming. They treated me like I was in some sort of curiosity show. Staring and jeering and trying to rile me. Can you believe some people?'

I shook my head. I couldn't get a word in

anyway, and I wasn't going to argue with a giant spider. Plus, it was good she was distracted. While she talked for Romana, I was able to think about how to free Flavia. I waved at the girl reassuringly, studying the rope of silk that had been woven around her waist, tying her to the net. She laughed and threw a thread ball at me. I swerved it but another quickly followed, thwacking me in the stomach.

The spider giggled. 'Would you like to play? We were about to make a silk rope swing.'

'That sounds lovely, but Flavia needs to come with me.'

The spider ignored me. 'I'm **Arachne**, by the way. I know who you are – I mean, I might live in the catacombs but I'm not totally in the dark.'

Arachne? No way – the first ever spider. And another one of Minerva's victims. Once a talented weaver girl, she was condemned to an eternal life of spinning by the mardy goddess, after they got into a barney during a weave-off. Seriously, that deity had a lot to answer for!

'Would you like a snack before we play? Flavia's having a sleepover. You're welcome to stop over too.'

A sleepover – seriously?!

'Can *I* have a snack?' said Flavia.

'Of course! One super snack coming up!' Arachne scurried down the wall. I braced, my whole body erupting in goosebumps. Talk about creepy!

'Nice to meet you, Arachne,' I said. 'Thanks, but I need to take Flavia back to her family.'

Arachne continued her journey to the back of the crypt, where there was a set of bowls set out on a stone altar decorated with skulls. 'I've not long made a fresh batch of oatmeal,' she said. 'I think there's enough for everyone.'

'Oatmeal?' Flavia sat up. Shadowing the spider's movements, she crawled across the net of webs, the rope she was tied to trailing behind her.

'Yes,' said Arachne. 'It's my favourite.'

'But you're a spider.'

'A vegan spider. Becoming the hunted kind of makes you re-evaluate things.'

Erg, like, hello! This was all very interesting, but I had a noggin to find. Arachne wasn't the only one of Minerva's victims still knocking about. And while what she did to Arachne was totally off the horror scales, the powers she'd given Medusa could bring the whole of Romana down. 'Flavia, we need to go now.'

'No,' said Arachne, slamming the lid back on her porridge pot. 'She's staying here with me.'

'But her parents are looking for her.'

Arachne rose on to her back legs. 'They'll be OK,' she spat. 'They have each other. I'm tired of being alone.'

She really was huge – her venom fangs almost the size of my arm. She might be a vegan, but she was built to kill.

'Well, maybe it's time to come up above the surface again, Arachne. You don't have to be alone.'

'What?! And have them laugh and jeer at me again? You have no idea what it's like to be me. They hate me so much they even invented a special word for it: Arachne-phobia.'

It's arachn*o*phobia, actually, but I could see where she was coming from. And I guess it must have felt pretty bad. 'Nobody hates you, Arachne. It's more, well, they're afraid. You have to show them there's no reason to fear you.'

Arachne's forehead crinkled.

'I can help you. Me and my family, we're a little different too. Maybe you could come and stay with us while you find your feet. I could share a room with my sister Poly. She's a cyclops.'

The spider's giant eyes glossed over like she wanted to cry. 'Really? You'd do that for me?'

'Of course. You can stay as long as you like. I'm sorry for what you've been through, but you can't just keep a little girl.'

Arachne looked over at Flavia. She shook her head and sighed. It was working.

'Danger!' Thelma's eyes flashed red . . .

. . . but she wasn't looking at Arachne.

She was looking back down the tunnel.

'Flavia?' called a panicked voice.

Anthony. And judging by the echo of hurried

footsteps, he'd brought the rest of the memorial party with him. They were going to ruin everything.

'Don't let them in, Thelma,' I said.

Thelma turned towards the tunnel, blocking the doorway with her arms. But she was too slow to stop Anthony. He shot into the ossuary faster than a sling-bullet. Catching sight of Arachne, he edged back again. His face ashen.

'See!' said Arachne. 'They hate me. I'll never fit in up there.'

'Poor Arachne,' said Flavia, dropping down from her perch. She undid the rope around her waist. It wasn't a restraint at all. It was a safety harness.

'No!' cried Anthony.

But Flavia continued towards the spider. I hadn't realized how little she was. Four or five maybe – the same age as Ari and Avi.

Anthony reached for the ceremonial dagger he was carrying in a pouch secured to his belt. Knife raised, he charged at Arachne. What did he think he was doing, the muppet! I grabbed his tunic, trying to pull him back, but the fine silk slipped through my fingers. Arachne rose up on to her back legs and raised her pincers.

I had to stop Anthony.

Now!

Unsure what else to do, I threw myself at him rugby-tackle style. Not pretty, but somehow I tussled him to the floor. All that play-fighting with Ari and Avi had clearly paid off.

Anthony looked over at Flavia, his body frozen as his daughter threw her arms around the giant spider and plonked a kiss on her furry cheek.

'Poor Arachne,' she said. 'Ignore those sillies. I love you and everybody else will too once they get to know you.'

I offered Anthony my hand. Helping him up was the least I could do after I'd taken him out like that. He smiled at me, and I thought about my own dad. How much I didn't want to share him.

But I also knew first impressions can be wrong. 'It'll be OK,' I said, as much to myself as Anthony.

CHAPTER 17

THE LABYRINTH

And right there, in Arachne's crypt, it *was* OK. The spider knew deep down she had to let Flavia go. She wasn't a bad arachnid, just a sad one. Her life had spun irreversibly out of control, and thanks to Minerva, she'd had a whole eternity to think about it.

Which is probably why she wanted to take her

time deciding whether to return to the surface or not. Giving me one of her silk balls to remember her by, she'd said her goodbyes and asked me to come back and see her after things had been put right with Medusa's head. Maybe, if she was feeling brave enough, she'd at least come to the surface for a holiday.

Poor Arachne. I felt bad rushing off on her like that, but we were so behind schedule it was unreal. She'd promised me she understood. She'd been wronged by Minerva too, and wanted to see Medusa find peace as much as we did.

The tunnels were narrower now. Colder too. I fought back the claustrophobia in my throat and chest and forced myself to keep moving forward. What else was there to do? We had to find Medusa's head. I'd made a promise. And it wasn't just Medusa who was depending on me.

Deeper and deeper into the earth we went, stumbling down roughly cut staircases, the tombs in these lower tunnels replaced by grey-white walls that reflected Thelma's spotlight. The glare made the blackness ahead seem even darker.

'Are you sure you're OK, Silvia?' asked Felix. Even in the dim light I could tell he'd been staring at me. Wondering why I was so quiet.

'I told you, Felix, I'm just missing Dad.'

'You'll see him soon. We'll all be together for the last few days of Saturnalia.'

'I hope so, Felix.'

'Don't worry, I heard him and Uncle Vulcan talking. He was really excited.'

'But that was before the ring. What if Dad wants to spend the holidays with Chitra and the boys instead?' I'd told Felix about the ring earlier. I thought it might help to talk things through, but it had just made my worries all the more real.

'Then they can come too.' Felix took hold of my hand. 'The more the merrier.'

I sighed. If only things were that simple. 'Are you sure we're going the right way, Thelma?' I said, changing the subject. I needed to concentrate on finding the head. Medusa's problems were far bigger than mine.

'Affirmative,' said Thelma. 'Light source ahead indicates our imminent arrival at the labyrinth.' She waved her pom-poms. 'Hooray!'

Like, no need! But Thelma was right about the light source. A warm yellow glow oozed from the far end of the tunnel. I pulled the balaclavas out of my satchel and handed one to Felix. Where there was light, there were people, and I really couldn't be doing with anyone else throwing themselves at my feet.

Wow! This cellar was something else. Its domed roof rose above us like a cathedral, a dozen narrow tunnels spiralling off the curved walls, evenly spaced like numbers on a clock. Painted on the floor, slap bang in the centre of the cellar, was a blood-red pentagram housing a charcoal brazier. Smoke drifted upwards from its roaring flames and disappeared into the darkness. Around the room, positioned either side of each tunnel, were a series of free-standing oil lamps as tall as Thelma. Their amber flames cast dark shadows on the cellar walls.

I followed Thelma towards the tunnel opposite. Unlike the empty black mouths of the other passageways, it was lit up by a welcoming glow. TIBI IUVET LABYRINTHUS, said the inscription on the keystone. *Have fun in the labyrinth.*

'Wow,' said Felix. 'I wasn't expecting it to be signed.'

Me neither. I squeezed past Felix and poked my head into the tunnel. *Proper fancy!* The wall brackets housing the dozens of flaming wooden torches were embossed with rubies and emeralds, and a purple and gold carpet runner stretched along the floor for as far as I could see. In between the torches hung a series of colourful Persian rugs and tapestries – more Middle Ages than Roman, like you'd expect in King Arthur's castle. 'There's something not quite right.'

'Everything is as it should be.' *Whoa!* Where did she come from? The owner of the voice was leaning against the wall just to the left of the labyrinth. In her hands she held a Rubik's cube, which she continued to stare at while addressing us, her fingers moving so fast they blurred as she twiddled the cube. 'Except, I don't recall giving you permission to enter. Back up now.'

Backing away from the tunnel, I edged closer to the strange creature. In the dim light, it was hard to work out if she was wearing a catsuit or if the fur that ran from her ankles to her neck was her actual skin. But her hands and feet were definitely human, her long, talon-like finger- and toenails painted bronze to match her eyeshadow. Golden furry wings jutted out from her shoulders, falling around her calves like a cape, and a serpentine tail unfurled behind her.

'The Sphinx,' I said. 'You're not what I was expecting.'

'You're not what I was expecting either!' she said, continuing to twiddle with the cube. 'Children? Is the Collectoris really so short of staff?'

The Collectoris? Mrs Burden had said there was no such person. But then she'd also said the Sphinx was dead.

'And what's with the silly masks?'

'They're a new security measure,' I said, glancing at Felix.

The Sphinx rolled her eyes. 'Always something with that one. The man's paranoid, I'm telling you – if that's what money does to you, you can keep it.' She glanced over at Thelma. 'I must say, it's a rather ugly curiosity he's choosing to add to his collection, but that's progress I suppose. Which is why I prefer to spend my time down here.'

'She's not ugly,' said Felix. 'You can't say things like that—'

'Ugly or not,' I interrupted, thinking on my feet, 'the boss wants us to deliver the robot to the vault as soon as possible. Come along, Thelma.' I mean, if the Sphinx thought we were here to do a delivery, I wasn't going to correct her.

Her mouth curling into a wry smile, she stopped fiddling with the Rubik's cube and handed it to Felix. 'Take it, child. The Collectoris was raving about it, you know how he is for his toys, but it holds no interest for me. The old puzzles are the best.'

Toys? Is that what Medusa was to this collector fella? Just another toy? I needed to find out more about him and his collection.

'I hear he has a new toy taking up his time?'

The Sphinx shrugged. 'There's always a new toy.' She stood up tall and pressed a bronze talon into my chest. 'And you should know better than to ask questions about them.'

Oops, bad move. The Sphinx was starting to get suspicious. 'Come on, Felix,' I said, shrugging her comment off.

But the Sphinx had opened her eagle-like wings and was now blocking the entrance. 'Ahum, where do you think you're going?'

'I told you. We're delivering the robot, and the boss is going to be very annoyed if we're late.'

'He'll be more annoyed if I don't do the proper checks.' She circled us, her inner lion far too close to the surface for my liking. 'You're not going anywhere until you tell me the password. You do have the password?'

'Of course.'

'Good.' The Sphinx placed her talon under Felix's chin and tilted his head, so he was looking directly into her eyes. 'Otherwise, I'd have to eat you. Not had a nice juicy boy for a while. The Collectoris keeps sending me girls because he doesn't like them. They remind him of his mother. What a nasty piece of work she was. Tasted good, though.'

Felix puffed up his chest. 'Eating people is wrong!'

'Shush, Felix.' I put my hand on his shoulder. 'Nobody's going to eat anyone.'

'Not yet,' said the Sphinx, licking her lips. 'So, the answer?'

'But you haven't given us the question.' We were going around in circles. And all that talk of eating children. Nasty or what?

The Sphinx's eyes flashed amber, her pupils narrow slits. 'Anyone sent by the Collectoris would have no need of the question.'

'We don't,' I said. 'But how do we know you are who you say?'

The Sphinx rolled her eyes. 'Aren't the wings and lion skin enough to reassure you?'

'The gods are known for their deceptions.'

The Sphinx wrapped her long serpent tail around Felix's ankle. 'Answer. Now. Or I eat the boy.'

Felix slammed the Rubik's cube towards her. 'That's not nice! You can keep your puzzle, you total Gaul!'

Oh my gods, that was it. The puzzle! The old ones are the best, she'd said. And the oldest and most legendary of them all was the puzzle the Sphinx had set for **Oedipus**.

'Man,' I said, trying my best to look disinterested. 'Or woman if you want to be a bit less sexist about it.'

The Sphinx tightened her grip on Felix's ankle. 'The full answer! Word perfect or you're barbecue: what walks on four feet in the morning, two in the afternoon and three at night?'

'Man,' I repeated. 'As an infant, he crawls on all fours; as an adult, he walks on two legs; and in old age, he uses a walking stick.'

The Sphinx stepped away from the entrance. 'Now was that really so hard?'

I shrugged. Who knew Dad's classics collection would one day save my life?

'See you, then,' said the Sphinx, sinking back into the shadows. 'Remember, keep going forward and don't open any of the doors. Minnie is in a foul mood today and I wouldn't want him to take it out on you.'

CHAPTER 18

THEY SPHINX IT'S ALL OVER

So much for the torches. What a con. They'd welcomed us into the labyrinth with their warm cosy glow only to stop as abruptly as Felix in front of a cake shop. Thank the gods for Thelma's spotlight. Without it, I could hardly tell if my eyes were shut or open. It was freezing too, proper freezing, our breath rising in wispy feathers that shone silver in Thelma's beam before drifting upwards into the darkness.

The tunnels were different here too: the tapestries and carpet replaced with smooth frescoed walls and mosaic-tiled flooring. The frescoes stretched from floor to ceiling: intricately painted scenes from history and myth punctuated occasionally by heavy wooden doors. I bit my lip trying not to think of what might be behind them. If they housed the same sort of residents as the Labyrinth of Knossos, it wasn't going to be pleasant.

The deeper into the labyrinth we went, the more the feeling of dread built in my stomach. Even Felix had gone quiet, distracting himself by softly humming the 1980s pop songs off the old cassette tapes Mrs Burden had given him along with the Walkman.

'Danger!' Thelma raced ahead on her wheely heels. 'Suspicious activity ahead.'

'What is it, Thelma?' said Felix, legging it to catch her up.

'Stay back!' The robot turned suddenly on her

heel, Felix slamming into her and taking her out like an NFL linebacker. The clang of Thelma crashing to the floor reverberated around us like a gong.

'Are you OK, Thelma?' Felix's lip quivered as he helped her back up on to her feet.

'Affirmative, Thelma is indestructible.'

Felix smiled. But then his eyes wandered to the adjacent door and his mouth fell open. It was slightly ajar, an earthy smell like cow fields radiating from it. The door creaked as I used the heavy iron handle to pull it shut. It creaked again and swung back open, releasing an icy draught that made my tunic billow. I gave it another go, but the same thing happened. 'Come on, let's get out of here.'

'Affirmative.' Thelma shook her pom-poms. 'Silvia is Thelma's friend. Best friends for ever. Let's play battledore.'

'Come on, Thelma. We don't have time for games right now.'

'Tuesday,' said Thelma. 'Time to squeeze your pimples.'

Erg, OK. 'Thelma, are you sure you're all right?'

Thelma's spotlight flickered. Her eyes rolled backwards. 'Two goats in a sack with a banana.'

'I think there's something wrong with her,' said Felix.

No flies on Felix.

'Do something!'

'Calm down, Felix,' I said. He didn't normally overreact to things.

And then I noticed it too.

The puddle on the floor.

Ichor.

'It's OK,' I said, placing my hand on Felix's shoulder. 'Thelma, can you kneel for me?'

'Orange peel.' The robot's spotlight had faded to a dull glow not much stronger than a candle.

'Please, Thelma. You have to kneel.' Removing my satchel, I gripped Thelma's wrists and pushed the back of her knee with my foot.

'Nits,' she said. 'Hairy nits.'

'Do something!' repeated Felix.

I pushed again. Thelma's kneecaps clanged like

cymbals as her legs buckled and she crashed down on to the mosaic floor. I waited for her to stop vibrating then parted her damp copper hair with my fingers. The cap in the control panel had come loose, and there was ichor pouring down her neck. Seriously, had Uncle learnt nothing since he made Talos? So much for being indestructible.

'Garlic sausage,' said Thelma.

The ichor warm and thick beneath my fingertips, I tried to tighten the cap. But it was no use. It just kept twirling.

'Maybe it's broken,' said Felix.

Another insightful comment. I wiped Thelma's neck with my cape and studied the cap. Her light had dulled even further but it was just about bright enough to see the crack.

'Powering down,' said Thelma.

'Thelma, no!'

Thelma's eyelids flickered.

Somewhere in the distance, I heard a ferocious roar.

And then everything went black.

CHAPTER 19

TWO, FOUR, SIX, EIGHT!

'What was that noise?' Felix grabbed my arm. Even though I knew it was him, I still startled. It was so dark in the labyrinth even Uncle Orcus would have been disorientated, and he lives in the Underworld.

'It's probably just the wind,' I said.

'Stop being like a grown-up. I know it's not

the wind.'

'Sorry.' I suppose I had been doing that white lie thing grown-ups do when they think kids need protecting. Felix was right to be annoyed. 'I don't know what it was, but let's just concentrate on fixing Thelma, hey.'

OK, I admit it. I kind of had an inkling of what the roaring was given the Sphinx's warning about some moody dude called Minnie, but saying it out loud would make it real. One problem at a time. Right now, I needed to sort Thelma out.

Which was going to be easier said than done – without the robot's spotlight, I couldn't see my own hand in front of my face, let alone what was causing the ichor to leak. But I could still feel the thick, warm liquid dripping between my fingers. I had to find a way to stop the flow.

The ridiculous balaclava didn't exactly help my vision. I pulled it off and threw it towards my satchel. That's when I remembered what was inside.

'My phone!' I placed my cape over Thelma's cap

and guided Felix's hand towards her. 'Here, hold this. Keep it pressed tight against her neck.'

The roaring again. Closer this time. Hands shaking, I rummaged through my satchel. Why did my phone have to choose now to play hide and seek?

'Don't worry,' said Felix. 'It's right there under your socks. It's so funny you can't see in the dark.'

Hilarious. And why am I only just discovering he can? Was seeing in the dark something all immortals could do or just another one of my brother's special talents? Whatever the reason, he was right. My phone was in the bottom of my satchel underneath the extra-thick socks Uncle Vulcan had insisted I pack.

'Ooh, bubblegum,' said Felix, his free hand brushing mine as he reached into the satchel.

The rustle of wrappers filled the silence as I waited for my phone to boot up. Felix must have shoved at least three pieces of gum in his gob. The gods didn't do moderation. I got the phone's torch on and passed it to him, then peeled back the cape.

'Shine it towards the back of her neck.'

'It looks like the ichor's stopping.'

Felix was right. The flow of ichor had slowed but there was a massive crack in the cap. We needed to seal it or the leak would just speed up again when Thelma was replenished.

'Urgh.' Felix pulled a face like someone had just wallpapered his tongue. 'This gum tastes funny. It tastes like—'

'Like . . . plumber's putty!' Oh my gods, that was it! 'Here, spit it into my hand . . . and get ready with the ichor can.'

Felix looked unsure but the slow, rhythmic clop of hooves echoing in the tunnel forced him into action. Fingers working faster than **Mercury** after he'd had his winged sandals serviced, I wiped the excess spit from the gum and flattened it like a pancake, shaking it to dry it off. Satisfied it had a good chance of sticking, I wiped the cap with my cape before covering it with the gum and working it into the crack.

'OK, fill her up,' I said.

The roaring again.

And the clip-clop of hooves.

'Hurry, Felix.'

Standing on his tippy-toes, Felix poured a dose of ichor into the hole in Thelma's neck.

'How long do you reckon until it works?' I said, screwing the cap back on and sealing it with the excess gum.

Felix shrugged. He placed the can back inside Thelma's hatch.

The roar again. So loud it made my eardrums vibrate.

I pressed Thelma's power button.

'Come on, Thelma!'

I pressed again, holding my finger on the slippery button until it hurt, but it was no use.

The roaring was right upon us now.

'Please, Thelma!'

Finally! The button flashed and the robot shuddered. Her eyes flickering, she lifted her head.

Mouth open, she began to make a noise like a stuck clock hand.

Click.

Click.

Click.

I slapped her between the shoulders. Not in a mean way, honest. But like you do when someone's choking.

'Who dares enter my labyrinth?' roared a voice so loud it made my tunic billow. 'Trespassers will be eaten.'

Minnie.

'You don't scare me,' said Felix. He squeezed around Thelma and stepped towards the roar.

He stepped back again.

And you would too if you found yourself face to face with a humongous, angry minotaur wearing a cropped footie shirt – Lazio, in case you're wondering. Tail swishing, the bull-headed cow man thumped his chest.

'Go away,' warned Felix, finding his brave again. 'Or I'll fry you!'

Minnie the not-so-miniature minotaur clawed the floor with his hoof. 'The boy has spirit,' he said.

'The spirited ones always taste the best.'

Holding the minotaur's stare, I let out a deep guttural war cry, just like the cry our LARP friends had let out when we'd stood against Bellona. It had helped us feel brave at Housesteads – the last time I was faced with imminent death – but this time there was just me and Felix and even he was looking at me like I'd lost the plot. We were doomed.

But then I heard a whirring noise. Thelma! She stood up and grabbed her pom-poms. 'Reboot successful!' she cried, waving them in the air.

The minotaur stood frozen in the beam of her spotlight. By the look on his face, he was not a fan of pom-poms.

'Danger!' cried Thelma. Siren whirring, eyes flashing, she charged at Minnie, kicking him in the chest. The startled minotaur fell heavily to the floor.

'Two, four, six, eight!' Thelma said, jumping into the air. 'Who do we appreciate?!'

'Thelma!' we all called together.

CHAPTER 20

OOPS!

We made the last part of our journey in silence. Nobody wanted to risk Minnie coming back and Thelma was running in safe mode. The chewing gum had held so far, but we figured it was best not to push our luck. Especially given we had no idea what we were going to come up against next.

'How much further, Thelma?' I said.

We'd been walking around in circles for hours now. And, yeah, I know that's a labyrinth thing, but it was still doing my swede in. Medusa wasn't going to be the only one to lose her head at this rate.

'Approaching destination,' said Thelma, picking up speed. 'Centre of labyrinth ahead. Proceed with caution.'

'Cool,' said Felix, racing to catch her up again.

I hurried along behind them. The tunnel was wider here. Taller too but somehow it felt even more claustrophobic. We were deep in the bowels of the earth with nowhere to hide and no way of getting in touch with our backup team if it all went wrong.

'Hurry, Silvia,' Felix called from up ahead. 'Look!'

Like, what? The tunnel was blocked by a pair of polished metal doors – the vault! We'd made it. But we were not out of danger yet. Who knew what surprises might lie inside?

'They look like those elevator things you have in

Britannia,' Felix said, staring at his reflection in the mirrored surface.

And they did. Other than the sun-shaped brass puzzle lock and the heavy hinges on their outer edges, the doors could have belonged in the reception area of any posh hotel. They had no place in the ancient world.

'Do you think Auntie Medusa's head is really in there?' said Felix.

'Well, there's only one way to find out.' I opened my satchel and pulled out the Janus key. It made a satisfying click as I slid it into the lock and turned.

Nothing. The door wasn't shifting no matter how hard I pushed.

'Thelma, you give it a shove.'

Thelma pushed so hard the heel of her bronze hand dented. But the door still didn't budge. I guess this is what happens when you're relying on a magic key thousands of years old. At some point, it's not going to be able to keep up with the technology.

Still, this is why we had the lava breakers . . . if I could only find them. Why did they have to be so small? It was like trying to find a needle in the labyrinth. The fact my bag resembled a rubbish tip didn't exactly help. I rolled up the scraggy tissues and sweet wrappers that lined the bottom and shoved them inside one of the socks, along with a lolly ice stick and a festering banana.

The breakers were right in the corner of my satchel, caught under one of the leather creases. I removed one from its protective case. It looked just like an orange Fruit-tella. Warming it between my fingers like Uncle Vulcan had told me to, I worked it into the crack above the lock. 'Stand back, everyone.'

The bubbling lava was almost instantaneous. It oozed into the keyhole and between the crack in the doors, crackling like popping candy. Happy we were all a safe distance away, I shut the lid of the case to trigger the detonator.

Bang!

So much for having fifteen seconds once I'd shut the lid.

And so much for the super-powerful explosives.

The shiny doors were now black from the viscous smoke that had filled the tunnel, but they were still very much in place.

'I'm not sure that worked,' said Felix.

I rolled my eyes. *You don't say!* 'You're going to have to open them.'

I know, I know. Mrs Burden had told him not to use his laser eyes down here, but the clock was ticking, and the lava breakers were about as useful as a balloon sword in the gladiator ring.

'Cool,' said Felix, a little too enthusiastically.

'You'll need to be mega careful though. There's not much room—'

But Felix wasn't listening. He was too busy running down the tunnel with his arms held up like he was about to spring into a handstand.

'For Romana!' he yelled, throwing himself forward into the air.

I shielded my eyes. I knew what was coming.

This time, the blinding light Felix generated when he shifted was accompanied by a blast of hot air. A blast of hot air that knocked Thelma and me off our feet.

'Seriously, Felix,' I said, staring through the dust cloud at the gaping hole where the doors had been. 'You were only supposed to blow the godly doors off!'

CHAPTER 21

THE GREAT HEAD HEIST

'Wowzer,' said Felix. Shaking the dust and fragments of plaster from his feathers, he folded his speckled wings and leant into the crypt beside me.

Wowzer indeed. With the dim lighting and pristine white walls, the vault was like a cross between a museum and Aladdin's cave. Glass display cabinets crammed full of curiosities lined the walls, and the lofty domed ceiling was home to dozens of exotic birds that had been taxidermized. Their jewelled perches swung in the aftershock of the blast. Positioned slap bang in the middle of them, sitting on a golden swing, was a fairy princess with long golden hair that would have made Rapunzel envious. Like the birds, she'd been preserved, her delicate wings stretched open, waxen face fixed in a blank stare. It was beyond creepy. How could somebody do that to her?

The rest of the exhibits weren't much easier to look at. At least not the ones in the giant gold-capped specimen jars: a little mermaid with blazing red hair floated in turquoise brine, while a wrinkled green alien gripped a potted chrysanthemum for dear life, and there, positioned right in the centre of the room on a marble pedestal, was Cupid! The mischievous love god was in his infant form, his golden bow drawn like he was about to shoot.

It was totally and utterly heinous. A collection

built of wrongdoings. But there was no sign of Medusa's head. Maybe she was in one of the display cabinets near the back? It was time to stop gawping and start walking. I adjusted my satchel and braced, ready to enter the crypt.

'Ooh, look at that,' said Felix, pointing at a glass case housing a leather and brass spyglass, an iron hook and a mahogany model of the *Jolly Roger*. He made to step into the room.

'No, Felix!' I grabbed the back of his tunic as the floor began to whir. Wow, Indiana Jones eat your heart out, cos this floor was proper booby-trapped – a kaleidoscope of polished brass panels and heavy clunking cogs moved and shifted in mesmerizing formations. Well, except for the panel by the door that Felix had stood on – that had fallen away to reveal a huge tank of aquamarine water.

'Sorry, Silvia—'

'Shush.' I put my finger to my lips. What was that noise? It sounded like honking . . . ?

Whoa! I covered my head as something

thwacked me big-style on the back of my neck.

Something feathery.

And loud.

A goose!

Doh! I knew it was a goose Albunea had drawn on her poopy scroll! They were everywhere now – the ones that had flown out of the crypt joined by a flock of waddling honkers who came at us from behind. Eyes black and wild, they pecked at my knees and ankles, honking like they'd just seen a roasting tin. Which, I swear, they would do if they didn't let me out of the doorway.

'Get rid of them, Thelma!' I called, batting the geese away.

Thelma continued to twiddle her pom-poms. 'No threat detected.'

Seriously?! So much for artificial intelligence. I got that the geese weren't exactly killers, but they weren't exactly onside either. I looked around for an escape, and spotted a raised viewing platform on the other side of the room. There was a flashing red light above the elevator-style doors opening on to it, and a goose was pressing what looked like an alarm button. It stared at me before flying across the room and dive-bombing my head.

'Thelma, do as you're told,' I bellowed. 'Unless you want to become part of this collection yourself.'

Harsh, I know, but Thelma didn't do subtle. And the threat seemed to work. Finally, she began to chase the geese up the tunnel, clapping her hands together like cymbals.

I turned my attention back to Felix. 'Right, you're going to have to fly me into the vault.'

'Cool!' Felix's wings fluttered in excitement. But then he looked at the whirling floor and his expression changed. 'But what if I drop you?'

'You won't drop me, Felix. You can do this.' I opened my satchel and took out the ball of thread Arachne had given me. 'But just in case, we have this.' Doubling over a strand of the super-strong silk, I looped it around Felix's waist like a lasso and tied the other end of the self-made rope around my waist.

Felix looked about as sure as a baby minotaur

taking their first steps. 'But I need a run-up. How can I do that with you tied to me?'

Mmm, good question. 'Hey, how about you give me a piggyback and then I'll drop down from your shoulders on to the rope when you take off. That way I can get closer to the exhibits.'

'Cool!' repeated Felix, his laser eyes shining red. He edged backwards down the tunnel towards where Thelma was still chasing away the last of the geese. 'Here should be OK,' he said, leaning forward so I could climb on his back.

'Wait! The goggles!' I put on my own safety goggles and then slipped Felix's on for him, taking extra care to make sure they were a snug fit. It wouldn't be much help to anyone if we found Medusa's head but were immediately turned to stone.

'OK,' he said, leaning forward again. 'Let's do this.'

It wasn't pretty – a cross between a leapfrog and a belly flop – but somehow I climbed on to Felix's back. I wrapped my arms tightly around his neck, hugging his waist with my legs – or rather what would have been his waist if he wasn't a giant potbellied bird with a human head.

'You stay here in the tunnel and make sure the geese don't come back, Thelma,' I said. 'And that's an order.' I patted Felix on the shoulder. 'Let's go!'

Felix began to run towards the vault. Well, when I say run, it was more of a waddle – the kind of waddle your out-of-shape uncle might manage when he's chasing after a bus while dressed as a Christmas turkey. But don't tell Felix I said that.

'Come on, Felix, you can do it!'

Reaching the entrance to the vault, Felix jumped into the air, his wings still partly folded so he wouldn't hit the exhibits. Somehow, his stunted flapping worked and we began to rise. Level now with the fairy princess, I dropped down from his back, almost taking out a waxwork of Queen Elizabeth II as we jolted forward.

Felix steadied himself. 'Can you see Auntie Medusa's head?' he said, hovering next to a glass cabinet containing a selection of jars and glassware—

Wow! **Pandora's pithos**! The clay jar was much smaller than I expected. How could something the size of a jam jar have contained all that evil?

'Silvia?'

'Oh, sorry, Felix.' What was I doing, getting all distracted by the exhibits? I needed to focus on the job. 'There's no sign of it. Let's circle the vault.'

Felix twisted himself round and flew towards the rear of the room, which was easier said than done with all the clutter as the leprechaun in rainbow-patterned trousers found out when I whacked into his pedestal and sent him crashing to the floor.

Or rather *through* the floor: the whirling brass panel his specimen jar smashed against sliding open and plunging him into the aquamarine water below. He floated there for a few seconds until the water began to ripple, a pointy-toothed eel breaking through the surface. The eel stared at me with its black eyes before taking a chunk out of the leprechaun's thigh and dragging him into the murky depths of the pool.

'Danger!' called Thelma from the doorway.

'We're fine, Thelma. Whatever happens, stay where you are. Do not try and enter the vault.'

'Affirmative.'

Arachne's thread digging into my ribcage, I scanned the glass cabinets.

'It's not here,' said Felix.

'It has to be. Try over by the viewing platform.'

'Ooh, look,' he replied, circling what had to be Juno's golden apple tree. 'Do you think you can eat them?'

Trust Felix to be thinking about food. The tree was pretty cool, though. On the floor next to it there was a velvet cushion with a pair of golden pruning shears resting on it. ALAN TITCHMARSH'S SECATEURS, said the engraved plate sown on to the cushion. Interesting combination. But not what we were looking for.

'Concentrate on the head, Felix.'

Felix let out a gasp, Arachne's thread shaking.

'I said concentrate.'

But then I saw it too.

The empty pedestal nestled in the nook next to the platform.

ILLA INCERTA, said the engraving. *The Undecided!*

CHAPTER 22

DANGER!

L*ike, what!* Arachne's thread vibrating like Apollo's harp strings, I stuck out my arms to steady myself, still staring at the empty pedestal. It was as though the vault was closing in on me, panic just a few ragged breaths away.

But I couldn't allow myself to be distracted by the empty exhibit stand with my nickname on it. I had to get this mission back on track. Not just for Medusa, but for Romana. I took a deep breath and pushed the image of myself drowning inside a giant specimen jar out of my mind. 'Focus on finding the head, Felix,' I said. 'Let's circle the crypt again.'

'But it's not here, Silvia. We've looked everywhere.'

'One last check.'

'Danger!' called Thelma from the tunnel. 'Abort mission!'

'Come on, Felix. Please.'

Felix tutted, but he did as I asked, stopping me in front of a cabinet containing the **Cap of Invisibility** – the very helmet loaned to Perseus when he sloped off to murder Medusa. Next to it was the legendary harpe sword which he'd used to sever her noggin. This dude really was quite the collector.

'Danger! Danger!'

There was a whooshing noise as the doors over the raised platform slid open. Felix wobbled again, knocking me into a giant specimen jar containing a winged monkey wearing an old-fashioned bellboy suit. Through the door appeared a man. A perfumed and oiled man with a seriously blingy necklace. He was wearing a deep red synthesis and leather falconry gloves, and had a padded vest fastened tightly around his chest.

No way! It was Crassus!

You remember him, right? The gobby dude from the senate who held up the sanitation bill? He was followed by a flurry of geese. Geese wearing . . . *armour*? Yep – brass breastplates and black-plumed helmets, to be exact.

'Well, fancy seeing you here,' he said.

I didn't reply. I was too busy staring at the black and ochre knapsack he was carrying – the **kibisis** – the special bag Perseus had used to safely carry Medusa's head.

This time it was my turn to gasp.

Crassus slid off one of the gloves and pressed his ruby-ringed thumb against a sensor next to the door. He flicked some switches and the rotating floor panels whirred to a stop. The armoured geese waddling behind him, he strode down the stairs into the crypt.

'Danger!' cried Thelma, landing with a clang as she leapt over the eel tank.

'No, Thelma!' But Felix was too late. The floor panel had already given way, plunging the startled robot into the tank below.

'Oops,' said Crassus. 'Must have forgotten to flick the switch for the sensors in that quadrant. Never mind, we can fish her out later—'

'You better!' said Felix, his eyes blazing red.

'Or what?' Crassus opened the kibisis. He thrust his gloved hand into the sack and pulled out a wreathing mass of coiled snakes, their skin a trove of muted rainbow colours.

Medusa!

And somehow her head was alive!

Alive, but definitely not kicking. Her skin was grey and wrinkled, hanging limply over hollow cheeks, and her eyes had been covered with a golden mask secured with straps like the ones on a horse bridle.

‘Help me,’ she said, her snake hair undulating between the straps.

And I would have, for sure, if I hadn’t been butted in the stomach by a goose.

‘Now, now, Nero,’ said Crassus. ‘I’m sure there’s no need for that. Our guests know better than to trifle with the master of the head.’

‘The master of the head?’ I cut the thread binding me to Felix with Alan Titchmarsh’s secateurs and dropped to the floor. ‘Medusa is her own master. Let her go!’ Glancing over to the harpe sword, I edged backwards. If all that goose waddling hadn’t triggered the traps over here, nothing would. Crassus must really have switched them off.

He clicked his fingers, and a flurry of honking geese took up position in front of the harpe sword. ‘I wouldn’t waste the effort. My elite Juno geese are trained killers. Plus, the sword is protected by a curse. You’re quite plain enough without oozing boils all over your body.’

I shrugged, trying to act like his warning hadn’t

bothered me. Maybe he was bluffing, but I couldn't risk it. The geese were pretty mean-looking and stranger things had happened in Romana than a case of oozing boils. There was only one thing left to do. Out-bluff him!

I folded my arms. 'Why don't you just make this easier for yourself and give me the head.'

'Give you the head?! I think we both know that's not going to happen. In fact, you, my dear, are going to succeed the gorgon as my most precious curiosity. I have a shortage of gods. They're particularly prone to escape. But as you can see from Cupid here, I've finally cracked the preservation process!'

Cupid blinked, an air bubble escaping from his nose. Oh my gods! He was alive! Preserved in a state of suspended animation.

'You're a monster.'

'I think you'll find *she's* the monster.' Crassus laughed and waved Medusa by the snakes. He placed a finger under her mask, tilting it just enough to expose the delicate skin below her eyes.

'A mighty fine monster too. Shame I have to give her up, but at least we had a chance for a little play first. Though I'm not sure my servants appreciated the game of peekaboo.'

Medusa's snakes hissed. They bit at Crassus's falconry glove, trying to break free. Rummaging in the folds of his toga, he produced a cattle prod and zapped the gorgon with it. The snakes screeched then grew still. I curled my fists into tight balls. It was time for Felix to use his laser eyes.

I knew it was a risk, especially given the mess he'd made of the doors, but what choice did we have? I squared up to Crassus. 'This is your final warning. Put Medusa's head back in the kibisis and give her to me now, or feel the wrath of Romana.'

Crassus laughed again. 'You really do think highly of yourself for a girl who spends her time dangling off an oversized chicken.'

'Why does everyone keep calling me the wrong name?' said Felix. 'I'm a *harpy*. A harpy with laser eyes.'

'And he's not afraid to use them.'

'Blah blah blah!' said Crassus. 'Guards, take down the chicken!'

A cloud of hissing, honking geese launched themselves at Felix, helmet first.

'Ow, that hurt!' He rubbed his neck with the tip of his wing. 'You naughty geese.'

Crassus smiled. A creepy, mocking smile that made the hairs on the back of my neck stand up. 'Well done, soldiers. Now deliver the girl to the preservation station.' He turned towards me and curled up his nose. 'She could do with a hose down before I pickle her. Her hair is terribly greasy! We don't want to contaminate the suspension solution, now, do we?'

The cheek of it! 'At least I've got hair.'

Ooof – judging by the way his mouth had twisted into a cat's bottom, Crassus did not like that comment one bit.

'Preservation station, now!' he hollered.

Waddling around a goose that had paused to lay an egg, the remainder of Crassus's spitting, hissing guards continued to surround me. Seriously, these

Juno's geese had major anger issues. I could totally believe their ancestors had helped save the Capitoline Hill from enemy invaders!

'Felix, do something!'

Felix's eyes glowed red. He squinted, eyelids opening and shutting like a nosy neighbour's curtains. 'My laser eyes are broken!'

'That'll be the paralysis draught my soldiers have just injected you with,' said Crassus. 'I do hope the arrows in their little goosey plumes didn't hurt too much.'

Paralysis draught? Crassus had to be bluffing, right? Mortal poisons wouldn't work on a god . . . but then I caught sight of Cupid. I had to take Crassus down now!

'Tragic really,' he continued, shaking his head at me. 'The legendary Undecided outwitted so easily. Athene Noctua was right – you're a total amateur.'

Like, what?! Athene Noctua was behind this? I knew the dreams had to mean something, but she was banished from Romana. I steadied myself against the nearest pedestal, my head whirling like the legendary pool of **Charybdis.** In the owl lady's hands, Medusa's head would become a weapon of mass destruction, for sure. Nothing would stand in her way.

CHAPTER 23

THE COLLECTORIS!

Focus, Livi. Focus. I fought back the panic burning in my chest. It was like the vault was stuck in some form of suspended animation. Even the geese had stopped pecking me. I had to do something. No way could I let Athene Noctua get her sneaky traitorous hands on Medusa's head.

'Thought that might shut you up.' Pushing a

goose out of the way with his toe, Crassus stepped closer. He lifted Medusa's head so it was level with my face. 'This little beauty is my ticket to godliness. In return for my loyalty, Athene Noctua will grant me eternal life and the emperorship of Romana. It is my wrath that should be feared.'

'She's lying to you,' I said, one eye on the geese, the other on the exit. 'She doesn't have the power to make you immortal.'

'With the gorgon's head and Athene Noctua's wisdom, anything is possible. The owl lady has assured me of such.'

'Well, she would say that, wouldn't she?'

'She gave me the Cap of Invisibility and the power to undo Minerva's spell and release Medusa's head from the shield. Why should I doubt her?'

The Cap of Invisibility – so that's how he took the amulet from Minerva's shield without anyone noticing. Nice move. Legendary, even. But I wasn't going to admit that to him.

'Erg, because she'll betray you,' I continued.

'Cast you aside as soon as she gets what she needs. It's what she does.'

Crassus yawned. 'This is getting boring. Enough with the stalling. Geese, seize her now. Set to work on the preservation process immediately.'

Erg, no thank you. Time to make my own legendary move, methinks.

But the geese had other ideas. *Ouch!* Felix was right, those tiny spears in their plumes really were sharp!

'The harpe sword, Felix! Quick – bring it to me.'

Felix fluttered his wings. Turning the colour of Roman cement, he plummeted to the ground.

'Felix!'

'Save your energy, dear, he's out for the count. Next time he wakes up he'll be inside a specimen jar. And so will you.'

'You calceus-licking toad.' Tiny spears stabbing at my ankles, I lunged at Crassus. A cloud of geese flew into the air, pulling at my hair and clothes.

Crassus laughed. 'Watch your mouth, girl! It's your own fault. You brought him here.'

Through the cloud of feathers, I caught sight of something shiny. The secateurs. I picked them up and flung them at Crassus. He wobbled as they struck him in the chest.

Oops. He liked that even less than the hair comment.

'Geese, fall back. I'm tired of her games.' Crassus raised Medusa's head in front of him. He removed the blinkers.

'Peekaboo,' he said.

Looking at the floor, I tried to edge backwards. But my legs were refusing to work. A wave of nausea washed over me. I hadn't felt this ill since me and my friend Mina ate four hot dogs at Jackson's birthday party and then went on the trampoline.

'Not so smart now, are we?'

My legs giving way, I fell at Crassus's feet.

'Look at her!' he demanded, holding Medusa's head above me. He knew as well as I did my safety goggles wouldn't protect me against full-on eye contact with the gorgon. I tried to squeeze my eyelids shut but they wouldn't work either. 'Look!' Crassus crouched down, his face blurring in and out of focus. 'Oh, you can't, can you? Neck a little stiff? That tends to happen with the paralysis draught. Never mind. Let me help.' He clamped his cold, bony fingers around my chin and turned my face towards Medusa. He pulled at the fastener on my goggles.

It was over.

But then I heard a howl. *Lupa?* A blur of snarling metal struck Crassus in the chest, sending him flying backwards . . . and Medusa's head rolling towards the gap in the floor where the leprechaun had disappeared.

'No!' Crassus cried, scrambling to his knees and throwing himself at the head.

The head that had stopped rolling and had somehow flipped itself over so it was staring right at him.

The head that turned him to stone, his face frozen in an eternal scream.

CHAPTER 24

REUNION

I don't remember what happened next in the vault after Lupa appeared and Medusa turned Crassus to stone, but I will never forget Crassus's petrified stare. Romulus and Remus said they couldn't stop thinking about it either. They'd arrived seconds after Lupa, just in time to see him turn to stone.

Yet it wasn't Crassus and his frozen scream that

was haunting me right now. It was her – Athene Noctua – and the thought of what was to come. I'd woken up back in my room at the temple domus, shouting out her name, and no matter how much Uncle Vulcan insisted the Fates were on our side, the worry worms continued to squirm. Even now, surrounded by my family in the brightly lit atrium, I couldn't get Athene Noctua off my mind. And I couldn't help but think that was exactly how she'd planned it.

The safety goggles didn't exactly help with the nausea, but it seemed wrong to keep Medusa in a smelly old bag, especially given how quickly she seemed to be failing. Uncle Vulcan had put her head on top of a marble pedestal in front of the family altar and covered her with a thin veil, so she had some privacy while she slept. Every now and again one of her snakes would hiss or squirm, but mostly she was deadly still.

Until, that is, Euryale and Stheno arrived.

'They're here,' cried Felix, rushing in from the garden.

'Mama!' squealed Poly, running along behind him. She pointed her stubby green finger towards the doorway where the gorgon elders were making their way into the room, Medusa's ghost speeding purposefully ahead, the trail of her long, elegant dress sweeping the floor behind her. 'Mama!'

'Mama?' Stheno's shrill voice echoed through the atrium. 'I don't remember having any children.' She wagged her finger at Remus. 'And you need a better landing strip. Hardly space to spread your wings amongst all that clutter.'

By clutter, Stheno meant Crassus's collection. Supervised by Tiber, the **Nereids** had been working nonstop to relocate it to the garden while we figured out how to return the objects to their rightful owners, and revive the living 'exhibits'. With a little help from Scylla, they'd even managed to fish Thelma out of the eel tank. Let's just say the eels were now sushi and Thelma needed more than a buff and polish.

'Pay Stheno no mind,' said Euryale, hugging Romulus. 'Stop complaining, sister, and pay your respects to our champion.' She took my hands in hers and kissed them. 'Hello brave child—'

'By Jupiter,' said Stheno, pushing Euryale out of the way and touching my forehead. 'The girl looks dreadful.' She turned towards Remus. 'Are you sure she didn't die in the vault?'

But Remus didn't answer. Not just because it was a ridiculous question but because he was too busy staring at ghost Medusa. She'd removed the veil and was standing in front of the pedestal studying her long-lost head. I checked my safety googles again as the snakes began to squirm excitedly.

Ghost Medusa seemed a tad excited too. Thrusting her shoulders back, she lifted her arms in a V shape and rose up towards the ceiling. There was a rush of hot air and the atrium was filled with a warm golden light. Shimmering dust mites floated around us, my hair and tunic crackling with electricity. The snakes screeched. And the golden flecks shot towards Medusa's severed head like iron filings snapping against a super-strong magnet.

Stheno let out a low, grief-stricken groan. Medusa's ghost was gone. Finally returned to the Underworld.

And it looked like her head wouldn't be far behind her. Seriously, that noggin did not look good.

'Sister,' said Euryale, making her way over to the pedestal. 'My dear baby sister.'

Shoulders slumped, Stheno followed.

Medusa's snakes began to squirm again. Fat tears ran down her grey, hollow cheeks. She thrust herself forward towards her sisters.

Stheno was sobbing now. Proper sobbing. She reached out for Medusa.

It was a beautiful moment. Or at least it would have been if Lupa hadn't run into the room and knocked right into the pedestal, sending Medusa's noggin thumping to the floor.

'I'm so sorry,' I said as it rolled towards my feet. What an absolute nightmare.

But then the head began to shake.

Medusa was laughing.

Euryale began to laugh too. She wiped a tear from her cheek and picked up her sister's head. 'Always had a strong sense of humour, our Medusa,' she said, smiling in my direction. She stroked Medusa's cheek, sadness darkening her smile again. Medusa seemed to be fading by the second.

'I am tired, sister,' she said through dry, cracked lips. 'It is time.'

Euryale nodded. She kissed Medusa again and turned to Stheno. 'Come, sister,' she said. 'Her final resting place calls.'

CHAPTER 25

ANOTHER WAY

Vulcan sighed, breaking the silence in the atrium. He placed his hand on Felix's shoulder and gave Euryale a sad smile. 'Are you sure about this now, cupcake?' he said. 'Only, you'd be much safer here with us. We all know this isn't over.'

Euryale folded her arms. 'It is over as far as I am concerned.' She nodded at Stheno. 'Sister, ready yourself. It is time for Medusa to return to Gorgonia.'

'But I haven't had me lunch yet,' said Stheno.

'Please, auntie, stay,' said Romulus. 'Let us talk this through. If Athene Noctua could provide Crassus with the means to reanimate the amulet, who knows what other tricks she has up her sleeve. We cannot protect you in the outer provinces.'

'My sister deserves to rest. I will not be dissuaded. Especially not by a scrawny, self-declared god who just a few months ago was puking up owl pellets. Now, where is the kibisis?'

'Can I at least have a biscuit?' said Stheno.

'Romulus is right,' said Uncle Vulcan. 'Athene's wisdom is pretty mythical. We must be ready for her. Has she tried to visit you again, Silvia?'

I shrugged. With the paralysis draught Crassus had used on me, I'd been so flat-out and groggy, I didn't have the energy to dream.

'Enough,' said Euryale. She took the kibisis from Felix, who had been using it to have sack races with Poly. 'I will see my sister find peace. I thought things might be different now, but once again history repeats itself – Medusa a trophy for those who wish to exert their power. I was a fool to hope for more.'

I glanced over at Medusa's head. It just wasn't fair. She'd been through so much. They all had. The gorgon people, forced to live a life on the edge through no fault of their own, deserved better.

'Do you know,' continued Euryale, 'I begged Jupiter to bring my sister back. To make Perseus return the head so the king of gods could breathe new life into Medusa. He'd intervened for **Psyche**. Why not my sister? Just imagine how different things could have been if he'd listened. If any of the gods had listened.'

Vulcan looked down at the floor. It was a good point, well made. Psyche wasn't the only mortal to return from the Underworld. And Uncle Vulcan had been as guilty as any of the gods in ignoring the wrong done to Medusa.

'No,' continued Euryale. 'It wasn't just Perseus

who wronged my sister. It was the whole **Dii Consentes.**'

'I'm not going anywhere without a biscuit,' said Stheno. 'For the love of serpents, what does a gorgon have to do around here?'

Uncle Vulcan sighed, the fire in the charcoal braziers fading. 'I am sorry,' he said. 'From the bottom of my heart. This is why I created Romana, to rectify the wrongs of the past. There had to be another way.'

'I believe you,' said Euryale. 'I really do, but there is no other way. My sister's continued fate proves that.'

I looked over at the kibisis, the story of Psyche swirling around my head. 'But what if there was?' I said. 'What if there was a way to right this?'

And take Athene Noctua out in the process.

CHAPTER 26

BYE BYE MEDUSA

It had a rugged sort of beauty, the island of Gorgonia. In the shadow of the clifftop caves, I studied the sparse cove below. Sea mist swirled around a shoal of wooden fishing boats, while gorgons carrying wicker baskets and clay urns scurried about the shingle beach like squirrels getting ready for winter. Adjusting the eyeglass, I zoomed in on the boats. They were decorated with garlands of wildflowers and floaty silk drapes that billowed in the wind. The sight of the biggest boat made my stomach flip. It was piled high with driftwood.

A funeral pyre.

The gorgons were ready to say their final goodbyes to Medusa.

All that was missing was the head.

That was still sitting in the temple on the cliff opposite, where it had been for the last three days. Yeah, I know, so much for not missing any more school. Thankfully, Uncle Vulcan had said he'd sort it. He tried to avoid interfering with stuff in Britannia, but we all knew there might not be a Britannia if I wasn't able to go through with this mission.

Which takes us back to Medusa's noggin. Good job it had already said its own goodbyes, I can tell you, because the temple it was resting in was little more than a domed colonnade. It must have been right draughty in there – kibisis or no kibisis.

Not that the whistling winds bothered the

mourners. There'd been a continuous procession of grieving gorgons travelling in from the outer islands since we got here. But the sinking sun told us it was now time for them to pay their final respects. The last of the mourners were making their way back down the steep granite steps to the shore and soon Medusa's legendary noggin would be little more than dust.

'Silvia, are you there?' Felix poked his head out of the dark mouth of the cave we'd claimed as our hideout. Behind him, Lupa's eyes glared amber. The metal wolf was already in flight mode, ready to spring into action as soon as she was needed.

'I'm right here, Felix.' Like I had been for the past three days, watching out for Athene Noctua. He just couldn't see me because of the helmet – well, it wasn't called the Cap of Invisibility for nothing. And it wasn't just my body that was invisible, it was my thoughts, too. So stick that in your beak and chew it, Athene Noctua!

'Can we go and get some dinner?' Fiddling with the dog whistle around his neck, Felix looked up at the sky. 'She's not going to come now. Not during the funeral.'

I wished that were true. But this was Athene Noctua we were talking about; the small matter of a funeral wasn't going to stop her getting what she wanted. I'd seen her looking for me in the space between sleep and consciousness. The anger in her eyes when she realized she couldn't reach me. She was coming, all right.

And when she came, I'd be ready for her. The owl lady might be the one known for her trickery, but thanks to Crassus's collection, I had a few tricks of my own.

'Sorry, Felix,' I replied. 'Remember what we discussed. You need to stay inside the cave with Lupa and keep quiet until I call you. And that means no humming. Especially the wolf song.'

He'd been humming 'Hungry Like the Wolf' by Duran Duran intermittently for days now. I cursed the day Mrs Burden ever gave him that Walkman.

'But Lupa likes it.'

True. She wagged her copper-wire tail whenever

he hummed it. Sometimes she'd howl along too, which might sound cute but should actually come with a noise pollution warning.

'She's bored, as well,' continued Felix. 'And we've run out of snacks.'

'Seriously, Felix, Euryale brought us a whole honey cake at lunchtime. How can you possibly have eaten it all?'

Felix shrugged. He put his dog whistle to his lips and leant back against the wall, his head nodding to the rhythm of 'Hungry Like the Wolf'. I couldn't blame him for being bored – it felt like we'd been on the clifftop for an eternity – but we had a job to do. We were only going to get one chance at this.

'Sorry, Felix, but you need to go back inside the cave.'

'But I want to watch the funeral. I've never seen Pegasus before.'

Pegasus? I turned back towards the cove. Sure enough, the legendary stallion was flying towards the temple, his winged silhouette black against the blood-red sun. On the beach below, the rest of the funeral party were making their final preparations. Dressed in dark wool tunics and garlands of purple bougainvillea, they loaded the boats with grain and olive oil – offerings to the gods to secure Medusa's safe passage.

Pegasus circled the stone temple. Landing on the narrow platform in front of the entrance, he folded his wings and nodded at Romulus and Remus. Well, you didn't think we'd leave Medusa's head unguarded, did you? The twins returned Pegasus's greeting and disappeared into the shadows of the temple, re-emerging a few minutes later with the kibisis. This was it.

Sack held firmly between his teeth, Pegasus turned to face the sea. Unfolding his mighty wings, he leapt from the cliff, his brilliant white coat iridescent. Shoulder to shoulder, Romulus and Remus watched him for a moment before beginning their hurried descent down the hill.

'I want to go with the twins,' said Felix. 'This is boring.'

'It's up to you and me now, Felix. We need to be ready for Athene Noctua.'

'But she hasn't taken the bait so far.'

'Shush, Felix.' We'd agreed nobody was to talk about the trap we'd set. Not here, where the sea and cliffs had ears. 'Stop acting like a baby and concentrate on what needs to be done.'

Huffing, Felix went back into the cave.

Checking my satchel, I turned my attention back to the funeral party. Euryale and Stheno had just placed the kibisis on the wooden pyre and the gorgons were clambering into their boats, the children carrying pretty, painted oil lamps to light their journey home once they'd said goodbye to Medusa in her favourite cove.

One by one the boats departed, following the lead vessel across the gently rolling waves. A slow, sad melody drifted towards me.

'Silvia?'

'What now, Felix?'

'I've tried to concentrate but the noise is putting me off! It's hurting my ears.'

'It's not that bad, Felix.' I wasn't much of a fan of the music myself, but it was a funeral, for Jupiter's sake.

Felix put his hands over his ears.

And then I heard it too.

A distant screeching that sounded like a cross between a very angry toddler and a demonic opera singer.

'Uh-oh,' said Felix. **'Striges!'**

CHAPTER 27

ROMAN FIRE!

'Watch out, Felix!' He'd almost knocked me off the cliff. It was my own fault, I suppose, for standing so close to the edge while wearing an invisibility helmet. But did he really need to run everywhere like there was no tomorrow? He was immortal, for Jupiter's sake.

'Sorry, Silvia,' he said. 'I was looking at the striges.'

Me too. There were shedloads of them now, swarming above the funeral procession. I zoomed in with the spyglass, and a shiver ran down my spine. Long and thin with round saucer eyes, they looked like little owls that had been stretched out on a torture rack. *Little owls? No! It couldn't be—*

'Hi-de-hoot-hoot!'

There was a tug on my helmet from behind. It clanged to the floor, wobbling precariously on the cliff edge.

'Surprise!'

Athene Noctua. Her magnificent plumed cape rippled in the breeze, the dramatically high collar framing her round face. Not good. We were supposed to surprise *her*. I threw myself at the invisibility helmet.

But I was too late. She'd already read my move. She kicked the helmet with her down-trimmed calceus and it tumbled over the cliff edge, crashing towards the sea.

She turned towards me and dabbed. Yes, I know, dabbed. It's one of her things. Along with reading people's thoughts and betrayal.

'Nice try, chick,' she said, 'but did you really think you could outsmart me? You might have been hiding behind the helmet, but I can still read you like a book. My extreme wisdomnous knows no bounds.'

Oh yeah, and bragging about her *wisdomnous*. That's another one of her things. Bellona might have used her powers to transform Athene Noctua from an owl into a long scrawny woman, but inside she was still that same insecure little bird with something to prove. I concentrated on the sound of the screeching striges. I couldn't let her inside my head. I couldn't reveal the plan.

'Aren't they just glorious?' Her feather-cut hair streaked with white, Athene Noctua eased in beside me like an old friend leaning in to share a secret. I edged away, hyper-aware of how narrow the ledge was. Shrieking striges hovered above and the turquoise sea loomed below.

'The mortals call them vampire owls,' she continued, 'because of their penchant for blood.

I've made a few little modifications to the basic model, though.'

Felix nodded towards the net we'd positioned just inside the entrance to the cave. The mythical net made millennia ago by Uncle Vulcan, so fine it was practically invisible.

'Don't even think about trying anything,' said Athene Noctua, her saucer-like eyes darkening.

Trust me, I was doing my best not to think about anything. I knew from experience she could read my thoughts before I'd even processed them. Without the element of surprise, we had no chance of our plan working.

'What do you want? Because if you don't mind, Felix and me are a little busy right now.'

Athene Noctua looked down her beaky nose at me. 'I think we both know the answer to that. The question is, how am I going to get it?'

The screeching was unbearable now. The sky black with swarming birds. Athene Noctua cupped her hands around her mouth and hooted. 'Team Strix, fire!'

A series of explosions broke the smooth surface of the sea, the water around the gorgon boats awash with flames.

'Roman fire,' said Felix. 'The striges are pooping it!'

'Like, how disgusting!' Though not as disgusting as the whole vomming up pellets thing. No wonder Athene Noctua had issues.

'Issues?' she said. 'ME? You're the one who shot her own mother.'

'But you have to admit, throwing up pellets on a daily basis kind of puts you up there in the minging creatures top ten.' Harsh, I know. Huge apologies to any owl readers, but I had to distract her somehow while I thought up a plan.

'Call that a distraction?' Athene Noctua shook her head. 'Time's up, chick. Tell me where Medusa's head is, or the gorgons get it.'

I shrugged. 'It's in the boat.'

'I'm not playing games here, Silvia. I know that's a pumpkin inside the kibisis.'

Oh yeah, sorry about that. I didn't want to

mislead you, but we had to keep everything hush-hush. Even the gorgons didn't know the funeral was a decoy. Secrets have a way of escaping. Especially when they are being pursued by a trickster mind reader.

Athene Noctua hooted again. Plumes of foamy water shot into the air around the gorgon boats. 'Now, tell me where the head is.'

I bit my lip. She'd find out soon enough.

'Take them out!' cried Athene Noctua.

This time the birds went for the boats. The shrieks of the striges were joined by the cries of the funeral party as the gorgons fled their burning vessels, young and old, fighting their way through angry white-tipped waves and plumes of viscous smoke to the shore.

We had to stop them! 'Felix,' I whispered, hoping Athene was too busy congratulating herself to notice me glance back towards the net. But Felix was kind of busy too. Arms held straight above his head, he bounced on his toes and sprang upwards into the air. Swallowed by the familiar blinding light that signalled his shift, he reappeared just below the cloud of vampire birds, where he hovered on his back, a magnificent flying turkey – oops, I mean harpy – a magnificent flying harpy that fired a string of laser beams from its glaring red eyes. Striges crashed like boulders into the sea.

Athene Noctua put her hands on her hips, her elbows jutting out like weapons. 'Serious wisdom-nous failure,' she said. 'Nice try, but my chicks are immortal.'

Maybe. But the soggy, charred-looking striges rising from the waves did not look well. Especially not after Felix blasted them again from above.

'Take that, stinky striges!' he yelled.

Feathers flew around us like an explosion in a pillow factory and the air was thick with the smell of barbecued poultry. Felix made the OK sign with the tip of his wing. I nodded and he zoomed up above the smoke clouds, where he performed a loop-de-loop before continuing towards the beach.

'You need to give your little brother a talking to,' said Athene Noctua. 'Nobody likes a show-off.'

Talk about pot calling kettle black.

'He won't be such a smarty pants when he meets Daddy.'

A shadow fell over the cliffside.

Uh-oh! The bird zooming towards Felix was the size of a passenger jet and it had claws like a road digger.

'Perfect timing,' said Athene Noctua. 'Let's test just how immortal your brother really is.'

I don't think so. I'd had enough of tests this week, thank you very much. Whistling for Lupa, I lunged for the net, a searing heat forcing me backwards on to my bum. I shuffled forward, away from the edge of the cliff.

Skin rippling like the lava soldiers whose power she'd harnessed the last time we'd come head-to-head, Athene Noctua placed the sole of her boot against my chest. 'Throw away your own life if you will, but do you care nothing for the pain of others?'

'Get off me, you big bag of feathers!' Pushing away Athene Noctua's foot, I scrambled on to my feet. I whistled again.

Finally! Ears whirring like satellite dishes, Lupa darted from the cave.

'Slow down, Lupa!'

But it was too late. The lollopy metal wolf charged over the cliff edge, taking Athene Noctua out in the process.

Which wouldn't have been all bad, I guess.

If I hadn't fallen over the edge of the cliff with her.

CHAPTER 28

MOTHER WOLF

Seriously, how many near-death experiences can one twelve-year-old have? How about I let you know if I survive? Which wasn't looking likely, given I was plummeting freestyle towards the sea. Ironic, really. Base jumping was on my bucket list – right after riding a motorbike in my guinea pig onesie – only I'd figured on wearing a parachute.

Follow your dreams, guys, because you never know what's around the corner.

Anyway, that's all the wisdomnous I have to share with you, except, maybe, never stand too close to a cliff edge . . .

Go on then . . .

. . . off you go . . .

. . . it's been a blast but it's time for you to look away.

THIS IS ABOUT TO GET MESSY!!!

At least that's what I thought. But then I felt a jerk from behind. Lupa! She'd caught hold of my tunic and was dangling me by the scruff of my neck like a mother wolf carrying her cub. Her tail whirled like a helicopter blade as she flew upwards above the fire of the striges.

I looked around for Felix. I couldn't see him anywhere, which I decided to take as a good sign. Especially since the giant bird had changed direction.

But then I realized why it had switched path.

It was flying towards me!

Not good. There was no way Lupa could out-fly the powerful strix.

Thankfully, Athene Noctua wasn't the only one with a surprise weapon. Looking the bird in the eye, I reached for my sword . . . the legendary harpe sword which I'd recovered from Crassus's vault. I know, nice move, hey! If the sword was powerful enough to bring down Medusa, it could sort this giant bag of screeching feathers out any day. I raised it up in front of me.

'Hold steady, Lupa,' I said.

But then I heard a ripping sound.

My tunic!

The bird hissed.

My tunic creaked.

I reached up, trying to grab on to Lupa, but my clammy fingers slipped off her damp metal shoulder.

The bird was right on top of me now, the metallic smell of blood pungent on its breath. I thrust myself upwards, finally reaching Lupa's copper-wire scruff . . . as the harpe sword went crashing into the sea. Instinct had taken over, and I'd grabbed on to the coarse wire with both hands. Doh!

Still, at least my tunic had stopped coming apart and my fate was no longer hanging by a thread. Literally!

Now there was just the bird to worry about. With its beak centimetres from my face, plummeting towards the afterlife was beginning to feel like the better option.

But then the bird froze. Its wings frigid, face congealed in a beaky scream, it dropped from the sky like . . .

. . . stone!

CHAPTER 29

SUPREME BEING!

No way!

Medusa!

It was Medusa who had taken the strix out!

I could hardly believe it either, but it's true. Uncle Vulcan had found another way. Despite his doubts, he'd done what Jupiter had refused to do all those years ago. He'd taken the gorgon's grey, withered head and brought Medusa back to life. Just like I'd asked him to.

Actually, delete that. It wasn't like I'd asked him to at all. I'd never have done that to poor old Medusa.

Cos you are not going to believe this, but he'd only gone and stuck her noggin on Thelma's body.

Fair enough, I knew the lack of torso might be a challenge, but he could have at least got rid of the cheerleader's outfit. Fancy waking up from the dead to find yourself in that get-up. It was enough to set you back a millennium.

Still, if anyone could carry it off, robot Medusa could. Her wrinkled face was now smooth and youthful, her snakes a multitude of gleaming rainbow colours, trailing magnificently down her back. Seriously, she gave a whole new meaning to supreme being. Especially with the super-cool sunglasses and the way she was handling Pegasus.

Snake hair flying, she gripped the stallion's gleaming mane with her robo hand and drove him forward. Closer now, they circled Lupa, Medusa expertly steering Pegasus into position below me, from where she reached up for my hand and guided me on to his back. Wrapping one arm around my waist, she charged towards the shore, baby striges falling like hail all around us.

Ideally, I'd have cherished that moment. I mean, it's not every day you get to storm through the air on the back of Pegasus with Medusa. But this battle wasn't over yet. Landing on the shingle beach, anger rose in my chest at the sight of the injured gorgons: young and old waiting patiently under rough woollen blankets to be seen by a healer. Parents comforted their children while others searched frantically for those who were still missing. The air was thick with smoke and pools of fire floated on the churning gunmetal sea.

Uncle Vulcan and Tiber had joined the rescue mission, working alongside Romulus and Remus to fish out those who hadn't yet made it to the shore. But there was still no sign of Felix. My feet sinking into the shingle, I climbed down from Pegasus and edged backwards. Medusa gave me the thumbs up, and Pegasus whinnying a goodbye, they took off again to join the rescue mission. But as much as I wanted to help too, there was something I needed to do first. If things really were going to be different, I had to sort out Athene Noctua once and for all. And to do that I needed to find Felix.

I whistled for Lupa, who was further down the beach terrorizing clumps of seaweed, shaking them with her mouth before throwing them into the air then pouncing on them. I whistled again and she legged it towards me.

'Where's Felix, Lupa?' I said, climbing on to a rock and scrambling awkwardly on to her back. Wolves were hunters, right? Maybe she could sniff him out or something.

The wind whistled around the beach. Lupa cocked her ear, her polished nose twitching. She began to run around in excited circles.

'Calm down, Lupa.' I patted her scruff, my other hand firmly gripping her grab rail. 'Go, find Felix.'

Lupa threw her head back and howled. Rising

up on her back legs, she thrust herself into the twilight sky. Maybe her training was paying off after all.

Except Lupa didn't go and look for Felix. Instead, she flew right back to our clifftop hideout.

'No, Lupa,' I said as she touched down on the narrow ledge in front of the cave. 'He's not here any more.'

Lupa whimpered. She twisted her neck and nudged my knee with her nose like she wanted me to climb down. When I refused, she threw back her head and howled.

'Hi-de-hoot-hoot!' Her cape swooshing, Athene Noctua poked her head out of the cave and dabbed. Seriously, when was she going to realize nobody did that any more? As for Lupa, she could get in the bin too. She may as well have handed me over to Mrs Dabby-Pants on a platter.

'Mrs Dabby-Pants?' Athene Noctua folded her arms. 'And don't blame the wolf for your own idiocy.'

Bile rose in my throat. And not just because

Athene Noctua was reading my thoughts, but because she was standing right where the net had been. With the Cap of Invisibility and the harpe sword gone too, I had no way to fight her.

'Correct,' she said. 'Game over. Once a loser, always a loser. You really are a runt. No wonder your father is building a new healthy nest with Chitra.'

A new nest – Athene's words hit me like a shot-put fired from a ballista. She'd always had a way of playing with my fears. But I couldn't let her get to me.

'Find Felix!' I repeated to Lupa. The metal wolf began to howl again . . . a howl that should have come with a noise pollution warning. How hadn't I realized? Felix was calling to her with the dog whistle.

I slid down from her back, hoping Athene Noctua hadn't realized either. After all, Lupa's howls were enough to drown anyone's thoughts out. 'Where's my brother?'

'Oh, cool your calcei. He's just running a little

errand for me. Such a good boy for Mummy.'

'Mummy?' What games was she playing now?

'Yes. It wasn't my intention, but with the striges gone I was a little outnumbered. I had to find a way to rebuild my nest. And the poor little chick, well he was just so desperate for a mother figure. The honey cake didn't hurt either.'

Lupa shook her head, her amber eyes flashing. She was right. Athene Noctua was squawking rubbish. Felix might like his grub, but he'd never betray our family. No way was he running an errand for Athene Noctua. So where was he?

'Family is fluid, chick,' she continued, reading my thoughts again. 'Ask your dad. He's already moved on and you know it.'

'Get out of my head! And stay out of it.'

'I'm just mirroring what you're thinking. The nest is full and you're the runt. Join me and Felix and we can build a new life together.'

'Erg, I don't think so.' She really was delusional. 'I'd rather vomit owl pellets!'

Athene Noctua rolled her fists into tight balls.

Her skin began to ripple.

Above the cave, I saw a flash of gold. Or at least I think I did. It was so brief I could have imagined it.

'Imagined what?' Athene Noctua stepped out of the mouth of the cave and looked up.

'You rotten meanie!' cried Felix, dropping the golden net on top of her. 'I'd never choose you for a mum.' He jumped down from the ledge and drew the corners of the net together, knocking Athene Noctua's feet from under her. Or at least I think that's what he did. I couldn't actually see him. Not until he took the Cap of Invisibility off a few seconds later. So, that's where he'd disappeared to. He'd been retrieving our kit.

But there was one piece of equipment he didn't need to recover.

I opened my satchel, and there it was.

Pandora's jar.

'Are you sure you want to do this, chick?'

I took the jar from my bag and prised off the stopper.

'You, me and Felix, we can be a family. The most

powerful family since the Kardashians.'

Like I said, delusional. I placed the jar on the ground next to Athene Noctua. 'In the cave, Felix,' I said. 'Now! You too, Lupa!' Legging it into the cave behind them, I clapped my hands three times and repeated the charm like Uncle Vulcan had told me.

Thunder split the sky in two and the rising moon turned blood red. Pandora's jar began to shake.

'You'll be sorry, you little vultures!' cried Athene Noctua. 'My wisdomnous knows no bounds!'

Was she really still going on? I covered my nose with my hand as a cloud of dust began to swirl around her. Growing bigger and bigger, it stretched up towards the sky, a huge tornado of darkness. Felix reached for my hand, and I wrapped my fingers around his, holding them tight. Every hair on my body was standing up and the feeling of dread was so strong I began to shake.

There was a bang, mightier than Jupiter's wrath, and the tornado mushroomed. It hovered like an atomic blast before re-forming and starting to whirl again. It was whirling far too fast for me to work out all the stuff that was now trapped in the dust, but from the screeching I knew the striges were in there, and possibly Mrs Burden's karaoke partner, Beryl.

I let my doubt join the dust devil too. Dad loved me. I knew he did. Despite my fears, I knew deep down there was room in our nest for everyone.

Thunder again. The moon bleeding red across the sky, the tornado began to slow. Athene Noctua made a sound like one of the striges, her eyes meeting mine for a moment before the last of the dust storm swallowed her again, dragging her headfirst into Pandora's jar. I rushed forward and slammed in the stopper, the pithos that had once released evil on the world now freeing Romana from the menace of the owl lady.

CHAPTER 30

PARTY LIKE A GORGON

Tunic – check!

Palla – check!

Ten packets of Turkey Twizzlers—

'Leave the Twizzlers,' said Dad. 'We need to go straight to the ceremony.'

'But they're Uncle Vulcan's Saturnalia present.' It was the final day of the festival – gift-giving day

– and I'd brought treats for everyone. With a little help from Chitra and the twins, I'd also made some special beeswax candles. They smelt much nicer than the cerei that were sold by the hawkers and exchanged at Saturnalia.

'You can give him them next time. He won't mind. I'm pretty sure he bought every pack in the big Tesco on our way home from Gateshead yesterday.'

I smiled to myself. Dad and Uncle Vulcan had gone to Gateshead to bury Pandora's jar. I probably shouldn't be telling you this, but it's now concealed deep under the foundations of the new Aldi that's being built there. Dad had been labouring on the site to earn a bit of extra money and it seemed as good a place as any to hide it. After all, no mortal could ever open the jar. Not with the special seal Uncle Vulcan had made.

'Come on, love,' said Dad. 'We're running late again. I can't believe it took you so long to get ready.'

Me neither. I'd been umming and ahhing about

what to wear. Going out in a synthesis felt a bit like wearing your pyjamas to a party. Still, at least I didn't have to wear a stola. They're far too impractical when you're riding metal wolves or fighting minotaurs.

Though I'd have happily worn a stola today. Today was mega special. As well as being the last day of Saturnalia, we were going to be officially recognizing the wrong that had been done to Medusa and granting citizenship to the gorgon people.

It had all been arranged in a bit of a hurry, to be honest, but everyone agreed Saturnalia was the perfect time for the ceremony. After all, it was a time of reflection and new beginnings; a time to say goodbye to the darkness and look forward to brighter days. Today really was a new start for everyone. Especially Medusa, who had agreed to take up an advisory role on the senate. She'd already been helping Romulus and Remus decide what to do about the sanitation bill.

'You look groovy, by the way,' Dad continued.

Groovy? He'd obviously been spending too much time with Uncle Vulcan. They'd been working on a new commemorative plaque for the senate house which was going to be unveiled today as part of the ceremony. We'd all agreed it was time to get rid of Minerva's shield. Medusa would still be watching over Romana, but this way she really could protect the city from evil. Trapped in the shield, her powers had been limited by Minerva's curse.

I slammed the door to the freezer shut and raced into the living room.

'Have you seen my coat?'

Dad shrugged. He was busy reading the invitation I'd placed on the stone mantel, next to the postcard from Harry Styles. Yes, *the* Harry Styles. He's a friend of the family. It's a long story . . . Anyway, back to the invitation.

The invitation to a wedding.

Mrs Burden's wedding.

Yes, seriously, I do not lie! Her and Bert were renewing their wedding vows. Apparently, they'd only had a small ceremony the first time round and after nearly being annihilated by Bellona, Bert had decided he wanted to finally give Coventina the wedding she deserved.

And it gets better. Because it turns out the engagement ring Ari had been playing with was Mrs Burden's. Poor old Bert had been too skint to afford one when they first fell in love after sharing a tub of cockles at Whitley Bay, and he wanted to make up for it. He'd asked Dad to look after the ring, which he was planning to give to Coventina today as a Saturnalia present.

And, yep, seeing as you've brought it up, I was feeling a bit silly about the whole engagement-ring panic. But what's a girl gonna do? Anyway, I had other stuff to worry about now. Like the fact the Burdens would be serving **lamb fries** at their wedding breakfast.

'Earth to Livi.' Dad waved his hand in front of my eyes. 'Are you with us?'

'Sorry,' I said, resuming the hunt for my coat. Dad still hadn't done the big tidy-up he'd promised, but at least the washing I found my coat buried under was clean and he had cleared space for the Christmas tree. It was progress, I suppose, but I had to admit I was more than a tad disappointed I wouldn't be having Thelma as a housekeeper after all. Still, I suppose Medusa needed her more than I did.

She seemed quite happy with having a robo body. She said people needed to accept her for who she was – snakes, wheely feet, and all – and the gorgons had always been different. That's why the myths had called them monsters, but hopefully people would now see it was their differences that made them special. Anyway, enough of me waffling on. Come and meet her for yourself.

Wow! Romana was buzzing. Like, seriously buzzing. We must have been later than I'd thought because the festival celebrations were already kicking off big-style. Thankfully, Romulus was waiting for us at the gateway in his chariot, all kippered up in a bright-orange synthesis with his snakes freshly washed and oiled. And it wasn't just him looking like a Starburst. Everywhere I looked, people were wearing their brightest garb. Even the shops and thermopolia were dressed for the occasion, the garlands that hung over the doorways and windows heavy with shining red berries.

The streets smelt different too, the air thick with the aroma of street food. Children munching on dates and walnuts greeted us with shouts of 'Oi, Saturnalia!' They chased the chariot into the forum where the festival was in full swing. And I mean full swing – acrobats, dancers, storytellers, it was all going on in the forum. As for the huge dance-off that was taking place around the basilica, there was a bit too much dad dancing going on for my liking, but people seemed to be enjoying themselves, so who am I to judge?

Those who were all danced out watched on from the sidelines, feasting on suckling pig and drinking sweet honey wine. Parents called to their children to come away from the rowdy dice games under the colonnades, while elders sat on the steps telling tales of those who had passed before them, ensuring the spirits of their ancestors would never be forgotten. It really was something special.

And the best bit of all was seeing the gorgons there; children and adults in their colourful goggles mixing with the city folk like they'd always lived side by side. It gave me that warm, fuzzy hot-chocolate feeling I got when I snuggled up on the couch with Dad on movie nights.

'Are you OK, sister?' said Romulus, directing the chariot towards the senate house. 'You are unusually quiet.'

I suppose I was quiet. I was busy taking it all in.

'It's just so perfect,' I said, catching sight of the **rostra** where Euryale and Stheno were sitting on intricately carved golden thrones chatting to Uncle Vulcan. The turquoise lace curtain hanging from the senate house colonnade billowed in the wind behind them, and the steps glittered with hundreds of oil lamps and candles that had been lit in honour of Medusa.

'The aunties were a great help with the preparations,' said Romulus. 'I hope you don't mind that they dyed the lace. It's Medusa's favourite colour.'

'Of course not,' I said. 'So long as Medusa is happy.'

Arachne had sent the webbing to me after I'd asked Felix to whizz into the catacombs and invite her to the ceremony. She'd said she wasn't quite ready for a big party, but she'd visit soon. If the gorgons could be accepted by the city folk, then maybe there was a chance for her too.

Medusa certainly looked happy. She was in front of the platform, dancing with Remus and Pegasus, my little sister Poly sitting up high on the winged stallion's back. Wow, those gorgons certainly knew how to party. I'd not seen moves like that since the *Strictly* final. Medusa looked like she'd always been a cyborg. Her refurbished head had quickly fused to Thelma's body, and there was no trace of the robot's clumsy awkwardness. She'd got rid of the cheerleader's outfit too. I think we can all agree that was a difference too far. And no, of course, she wasn't in the nuddy. What are you like? I know it's different rules for robots, but come on.

Seeing as you asked, she was wearing a floaty turquoise dress, the special sunglasses Uncle Vulcan had made to ensure she didn't turn anyone to stone secured with a matching ribbon that had been woven under her snakes. Which were looking truly magnificent in all the colours of Saturnalia. I still couldn't get over how youthful she looked. Even her fangs looked whiter. Forget the fountain of youth, soaking your head in nectar was clearly the way to go.

Climbing down from the chariot, I smiled at the sight of Tiber and Felix, who were standing on the other side of the platform, swaying to the music while stuffing fried-meat sandwiches into their gobs. Tiber was carrying baby Bellona in her sling, Felix proudly in charge of rocking Scylla's special tank-pram – a blingy contraption Vulcan had made so she could shrink down and join the rest of the family on days out. Above their heads fluttered Cupid, who was lobbing grapes at the crowd. He'd been nothing but trouble since Tiber had freed him from his jar. Though after Uncle Vulcan had confiscated his bow and arrow as punishment for making Bert fall in love with a chicken, he'd had to find new ways to make mischief.

Come on, we can say hello to that lot in a minute. First, I need to say '**Io Saturnalia**' to Stheno and Euryale.

'Silvia,' said Euryale, kissing me on both cheeks. 'Io Saturnalia to you too! Isn't it wonderful. Everyone is having such a lovely time.'

'Finally put in an appearance, 'ave yer?' said Mrs Burden. Where did she come from? She was wearing a forest-green synthesis and smelt extra strong of mountain springs. 'Do you think we've not got anything better to do than wait around 'ere for you?'

I looked over at the giant hourglass that had been placed next to the thrones, counting down to the unveiling of the plaque. The last few grains of sand were trickling into the bottom bulb.

'Perfect timing,' said Stheno, more to annoy Mrs Burden than stick up for me. They hadn't been speaking since Kevin chewed Stheno's sandal and she'd threatened to give him a flea treatment he'd never forget.

Anyway, what was Mrs Burden's problem? It's not like I was doing the unveiling. That would have been wrong. Today was about Medusa and the gorgons. Which is why I'd suggested Romulus and Remus unveil the plaque. Plus, I really didn't like the whole public speaking thing. I might be a mythical hero, but I was still only twelve.

Remus, on the other hand, loved all that stuff. He was already standing on the rostra with his scroll, reading through his speech. He signalled for Romulus to join him. Judging by the length of the scroll this was going to take a while . . .

. . . for ever, in fact.

Well, it felt like for ever. It wasn't quite as bad as waiting for Albunea to come out of one of her bird-poo trances, but it was still pretty grim. Probably on a par with having to listen to the King's Speech on Christmas Day when all you want to do is eat Quality Street and play with your presents.

Although the crowd seemed to enjoy it. Their cheering was so loud it woke me back up from my daydream. Which, quite frankly, was a bit annoying, because I was in the middle of imagining I owned an ice cream parlour—

'Silvia.' Dad nudged me gently with his hip. 'Go on.'

Erg, what? What did he mean go on? I *so* wasn't listening.

'They want you to remove the veil.'

'Come, sister,' called Remus. 'None of this would have been possible without the great Undecided.'

The cheering grew louder.

'*There's only one Undecided*,' chanted the crowd. '*One Undeciiiiided!*'

The colour rising in my cheeks, I made my way towards my brothers, who were standing either side of Medusa. She rummaged in her bag – the refurbished kibisis – and pulled out Thelma's pom-poms.

'Give us an S!' she said, shimmying her shoulders

and raising them into the air.

'Give us an I!' She twirled the pom-poms.

'Give us an L—'

Fast forward. You know where this is going . . .

. . . except, that is, for the part where the whole crowd joined in. Jumping into the air as one and yelling, 'Silvia!'

Embarrassing or what! My cheeks were burning like I'd just had a ride in Sol's chariot. Though it was kind of nice to be appreciated.

Waiting for the crowd to calm, I joined Romulus and Remus and took hold of one of the tasselled cords attached to the lace curtain. We counted down together. 'One potato, two potato, three potato, go!' And there it was. A gleaming, golden symbol of the future. Nice job, Dad and Uncle Vulcan.

Not that most of the crowd could see the plaque under the colonnade, but that didn't stop them cheering. Those that could see it were presented with an intricate engraving of Medusa, riding high across the sun on Pegasus. Below her, Uncle Vulcan had scored tiny likenesses of me and my family: the Prima Gorgons standing in the middle of the group, everyone linking arms. It would be a constant reminder of our new beginning. The gorgons no longer had to live on the margins and Romana was free once and for all from Athene Noctua.

Of course, that's not to say everything was going to be smooth sailing. Trouble always seemed to be simmering in Romana, and there was still the matter of the Burdens' lamb fries to contend with. But whatever this new year brought, we'd face it together. United.

Meanwhile, the Saturnalia celebrations called. It was time to go and dance with Auntie Medusa.

GLOSSARY

AMBROSIA a god's favourite scran. In Romana, served as a cake.

ARACHNE defiant mortal turned into a spider by Minerva because she upset her during a weave-off. You are going to ask me who Minerva is now, aren't you?

AUGURY looking for clues about the future – *omens* – in the behaviour of birds.

AUREUS (PLURAL 'AUREI') gold coin used across the Roman Empire until Constantine shook things up in 312 CE.

BASILICA one of the fancy buildings you'll find in the forum. A bit like your town hall crossed with the city law courts with some shops thrown in for good measure.

CALCEUS (PLURAL 'CALCEI') Roman equivalent to a walking boot. Made your feet smelly in warmer parts of the empire, so sandals or open-toed boots were preferred there.

CAP OF INVISIBILITY one of several names for the legendary helmet Perseus wore when he slayed Medusa. Made the little sneak invisible, so poor old Medusa had no chance against him.

CHARYBDIS legendary sea monster dwelling off Sicily. Beware the whirlpool she belches up three times a day. Nice.

CONSUL the two big cheeses on the senate who shared the highest position in government.

COVENTINA the goddess of lamb fries. Only kidding. She's the Celtic goddess of wells and springs, and one of the many local gods adopted by the Romans because they liked to hedge their bets.

CRASSUS yes, there really was a super-rich Roman consul called Marcus Licinius Crassus (115–53 BCE), and yes he really was known for playing political games.

DII CONSENTES the big cheeses when it came to gods. Or the twelve most important deities of the Roman pantheon, if you want to be posh about it.

DOMUS a Roman home or dwelling – in this case, a proper posh one.

FATES, THE or rather the *parcae*, as they were known in Ancient Rome. The masters of your destiny – Old Nona, Decuma and Morta mapped out your life at birth, even deciding when you'd die. Yeah, right.

FESTINA LENTE Latin phrase translating as *make haste slowly*. It basically means you shouldn't rush when doing something important, but should give yourself time to think it through.

FORTUNA the goddess of fortune. Depending on her mood, she might bring good or bad luck. Best hope she's in a good mood before your next test.

FORUM the place to be in Ancient Rome if you want to go shopping, hang out with your mates, do business or sacrifice a bull. It's all happening at the forum!

FRESCO (PLURAL 'FRESCOES') Roman wall painting. Paint is applied when the plaster is wet, which makes it part of the wall's surface.

HADRIAN'S WALL very long wall built by the Roman emperor Hadrian across northern Britannia. It runs from what is now Tyne and Wear to western Cumbria, and was built to keep the Caledonians out cos they were harder than the Romans.

HARPY I could tell you what a harpy is but that will ruin the surprise when Felix turns into one.

HOSPITIUM the divine duty of hospitality. Be nice to your guests or, for that matter, total strangers who just turn up at your door – or feel the wrath of the gods!

IMPLUVIUM a pool usually found in the main room of a Roman house, used to catch rainwater off the open sloping roof. And, yep, it is about time Uncle Vulcan built some aqueducts – fresh drinking water piped into the city being much preferred by your average Roman.

IO SATURNALIA festive greeting shared at Saturnalia. The *io* is pronounced *yo*, which rhymes with *ho*, causing the dudes up the road at the Vindolanda museum to suggest it might have been where Santa got his 'ho ho ho' from.

JANUS Roman god of doorways and transitions. Had two faces – one looking forward to the future, the other back to the past.

JANUS-FACED a rather witty spin on the expression 'two-faced', even if I do say so myself. What? You don't get it? Well, may I suggest you look up Janus?

JUNO'S GEESE the sacred geese who supposedly saved Rome from a stealth invasion by the Gauls when they honked a warning to the sleeping residents of the Capitoline Hill.

KIBISIS the mythical sack in which that scoundrel Perseus carried Medusa's noggin.

LABYRINTH think maze except with a single winding path leading to the centre. Though just to complicate things, the labyrinth at Knossos probably was a maze, the terms often used interchangeably. Confusing or what?

LAETITIA goddess of joy, gaiety and celebration. May have been a minor deity but at least she knew how to have a good time.

LAMB FRIES I told you in the last book you don't want to know what these are. Google at your own peril.

LARP OR LIVE-ACTION ROLE-PLAY a role-playing game where you dress up as your chosen character and act out the game. There are lots of types of LARP, including high fantasy, zombie or alien invasions or, yes, even Ancient Rome. Mine and Dad's favourite pastime.

LECTUS Ancient Roman bed or couch, or both, depending on your preferences. Used for sitting, sleeping, chilling and eating your tea on.

MANICA an arm guard often made of overlapping leather or metal plates. You've seen the pics of the gladiators with their huge sleeves, right, so you'll know exactly what I mean.

MERCURY busy old god with a range of roles, but perhaps most famous for his winged sandals and importance to travellers and merchants. Watch him, though – he's also the god of tricksters and thieves.

MINERVA Roman goddess of wisdom, the arts, strategic warfare and a load of other stuff including weaving. Athene Noctua's former master, she's just as conceited and annoying.

NECTAR the gods' favourite liquid refreshment. Drink it with ambrosia cake to top up your godliness.

NEREIDS mythical sea nymphs and Vulcan's right-hand women.

OEDIPUS Greek tragic hero who outwitted the Sphinx of Thebes.

OSSUARY room or container housing human bones. The Romanan ossuaries described here are inspired by the Paris catacombs – Bellona not being one to be outdone by the Gauls.

PALLA a posh cloak typically worn by married women of status in Ancient Rome but which any old Romanan is free to wear.

PANDORA'S PITHOS yes, pithos. I know you thought it was a box Pandora opened, releasing all that evil into the world, but it was a jar. Take my word for it – my Uncle Vulcan crafted Pandora after all.

PANTHEON a super-famous temple. Built over 2,000 years ago, it is one of the best-preserved buildings from Ancient Rome and a brilliant example of fancy-pants Roman concrete work.

PEGASUS of course you've heard of Pegasus. But did you know he was Medusa's son? He sprang from her neck, along with the giant Chrysaor, when Perseus chopped off her noggin.

PILEUS (PLURAL 'PILEI') pointy felt hat usually worn by freedmen but worn by all during Saturnalia, when the enslaved were given greater freedoms and the Romans liked to pretend everyone was equal.

PORTICO a columned walkway or porch you'll find on a lot of Roman buildings. Go up the temple steps through the columns and, hey presto, you are hanging in the portico.

PSYCHE or Anima. Another mythical mortal wronged by a vain and spiteful goddess. Only this time Jupiter stepped in, told Venus to wind her neck in and made Psyche immortal.

ROMAN FIRE more commonly known as Greek fire, a weapon used in naval warfare that released a substance that burnt on water.

ROSTRA raised platform in the Roman forum used for public speaking. Often occupied by waffling politicians. It's where the word 'rostrum' originates from.

SATURNALIA don't worry, you'll learn all about the biggest festival of the Ancient Roman year throughout this book. Meanwhile cool your calcei.

SENATE the literal meaning is 'gathering of old men'. Its 300-plus elected senators governed Rome during the Republic, but had their powers much reduced during imperial times, when the emperor liked to be top dog! Woof!

SIBYL OF TIBURTINE, THE also known as Albunea. The Sibyl of Tiburtine, according to Christian tradition, was a famous prophetess who predicted the birth of Jesus Christ.

SIBYLLINE BOOKS proper big scrolls containing prophecies that the Romans consulted when they had a major problem and no clue what to do.

SIGILLARIA mini wax or pottery figures exchanged as gifts during Saturnalia.

SOMNUS Roman god of sleep. Yawned a lot. Oh no, wait, that's me.

SPHINX OF THEBES meanie lion-woman with wings who guarded the City of Thebes. Get her riddles wrong and she'll eat you. Owp!

STRIX (PLURAL 'STRIGES') seriously nasty mythological bird with a big head, said to have a fondness for drinking blood.

SYNTHESIS a colourful robe or garb normally preserved for private dining, but at Saturnalia it was synthesis all the way with everyone going around in their brightly coloured house clothes.

TALOS a giant robot-bloke built by my Uncle Vulcan to protect the island of Crete.

TERRA big cheese goddess said to be earth personified. Not quite sure how that's possible, but anyway, she's been around for, like, ever and had shedloads of mythical children.

TOGA PULLA dark-coloured toga worn at posh funerals or when mourning other posh people.

VICTORIA goddess of victory. Which is probably why she was a favourite of the Roman military. Had ideas above her station, according to Bellona.

ACKNOWLEDGEMENTS

Quick, look away, because this is about to get soppy. You see, this book is dedicated to my husband Mark and son Dylan, and I'm about to tell them how much I love them. Yeah, yuck. But without these mythic heroes, there would be no books by Marie Basting. They lift me up – think Atlas but without the muscles – and support me on whatever foolish quest I decide to undertake. Yes, there is no harder critic than Dylan – trust me, I have the scars to prove it – but there is no fairer champion either. From the very first moment I put pen to paper, he talked only of *when* I became an author and never *if*. Not once did he doubt me.

And good old Mark had such faith in my abilities he didn't even bat an eyelid when I gave up a perfectly good career to swan about in imaginary worlds making friends with teabags. Thank you both so much! Cupid's arrow has no stronger spell than the one I am under when it comes to you. Now go and make me a cup of tea or something before I make everyone sick.

Next up in the Marie Love Parade are my godly editor Ronnie-Rachel-Shirley Leyshon and deific agent Kate Shaw. Thank you, *Shirl*, for your divine guidance and inspiration, and for making the whole process of writing this book such fun. I couldn't think of a better editor to go on a quest with. And Kate, thank you for being the voice of reason and calm, and for being there to light my way through the publishing labyrinth with your glorious aura. You are my Minerva but without the bad bits.

Rome wasn't built in a day, and, likewise, behind every great book there is a brilliant publishing team working their woolly socks off relentlessly. A huge thank you to the mythical team at Chicken House Books: Barry Cunningham, Rachel Hickman, Laura Myers, Elinor Bagenal, Megan Farr, Ruth Hoey, Laura Smythe, Jazz Bartlett Love, Emily Groom-Collis, Esther Waller and Shalu Vallepur. Could there be a better team to have behind me? Erg, no! Thanks also to copy-editor Fraser Crichton, proofreader Sara Magness and Latin guru Nicholas Bowling.

If you are still here, can you please drop down on your knees in honour of cover illustrator Flavia Sorrentino? Flavia, thank you so much, I think this could be my favourite cover yet and I almost cried when I saw the chapter headers. In a good way, obviously. You are truly divine and if I could designate your birthday a feast day and make it even bigger than Saturnalia, I would. Thanks also to cover designer Steve Wells for adding an extra layer of magic.

A huge thank you must also go to the divine writing friends who have supported me over the course of writing this book: the Swaggers, Foresters, Furies, Juvenile Litters, SCBWIers and all the authors and illustrators I've been lucky enough to befriend on my writing journey. While I would sacrifice a bull for any of you – or at least a chicken – particular thanks must go to Lou Cliffe-Minns, Danielle Jawando and the wonderful Swaggers – nectar and ambrosia all round!

The children's book community is an amazing

thing to be part of and I am so grateful to everyone who has advised, supported and championed me. Key to that community, of course, are the wonderful bloggers, librarians, booksellers, festival staff, teachers and literacy advocates who work so hard to encourage reading for pleasure and get our books into the hands of readers. I raise a glass of nectar to you all. Particular thanks to the team at the Portico Library, Urmston Book Shop and BooksForTopics. And no, not just because BooksForTopics awarded me my first writing trophy. How dare you!

And, of course, thanks also to all the friends and family who have continued to cheer me on from the sidelines, especially Mum and Dad who NEVER miss a Facebook post and will happily tell you how wonderful I am if you forget. A special shout-out, too, for my own awesome aunties, each and every one as special as Medusa. We miss you, Auntie Irene, and I thought of you often when writing this book.

A big thank you also to the classics and history

community who have embraced this book and to their Greco-Roman forefathers for inspiring me. Homer, Virgil and Ovid, you rock!

And, finally, thanks to YOU the reader for coming along on this journey with me. I get so much joy from meeting readers at events and school visits and I hope to meet many more of you soon! Meanwhile, stay awesome and keep tight hold of your noggin!